A Pictorial Guide to the Big Blue Poppies (Meconopsis)

by
Evelyn Stevens
2015

About the Author

Evelyn Stevens is a zoologist by training but has had a life-long interest in plants. In 1985 she and her husband bought a derelict farmhouse in central Scotland with 3½ acres of land in which they developed a garden, latterly specialising in *Meconopsis* and snowdrops. She has been a member of the Scottish Rock Garden Club since 1979 and Secretary from 1985 to 1991. In 1998 she co-founded The Meconopsis Group. From 2001 to 2015 she held a National Collection of *Meconopsis*. She has received the Clarence Elliot Memorial Award and the Kath Dryden Award from the Alpine Garden Society, the Brickell Award from the National Council for the Conservation of Plants and Gardens, and the Dr Patrick Neill Award from the Royal Caledonian Horticultural Society. She has published a number of articles in The Rock Garden, The Plantsman, Sibbaldia and The Alpine Gardener, and her garden has featured on two television gardening programmes.

Front cover: *Meconopsis* 'Jimmy Bayne' (photograph: Jim Smith).
Back cover: A view in the author's garden including various *Meconopsis*.

Published by Dander Publishing
16 Valmont Road, Bramcote, Nottingham NG9 3JL

ISBN: 978-0-9562168-1-6

Book design and layout by Patricia Lewis (www.lewiscreative.co.uk)
Printed and bound in the UK by Biddles, Kings Lynn PE3 1SF (www.biddles.co.uk)

Preface

At the beginning of the last century, blue poppies (*Meconopsis*) were introduced to Western Europe from the Himalayas, western China and south-eastern Tibet. In cultivation during the course of the twentieth century they hybridised in gardens to produce a range of beautiful plants now known as the Big Perennial Blue Poppies. This book describes and illustrates the variety of these *Meconopsis* in cultivation. It should enable the reader to appreciate the attraction of these plants, distinguish different cultivars and understand the conditions needed to grow and propagate them.

Meconopsis have the reputation for being difficult to grow. Therefore there is a section with information and advice on the conditions needed to grow and propagate them. Also listed are gardens where a good selection of *Meconopsis* can be seen, including the Plant Heritage National Collections, and for those wishing to grow them in their own gardens, where to obtain them.

The illustrations are carefully chosen to show the characteristic features of each cultivar at different stages of its life cycle. These include the emergence of the leaves in early spring, the development of the flowering stem, the appearance of the flowers and finally the formation of the fruit capsules. The characterisation of the large number of cultivars has been possible as a result of research carried out by the author since the early 1980s and along with The Meconopsis Group since the late 1990s.

Evelyn Stevens
Sheriffmuir
August 2015

Acknowledgements

It gives me much pleasure to express my indebtedness to the many *Meconopsis* enthusiasts whose zeal for these plants, their help and their involvement have contributed to make this book possible. First there was my builder friend, the late Jimmy Bayne, where it all started with the gift of what became *Meconopsis* 'Jimmy Bayne', and then the late Mervyn Kessell who first suggested forming a study group, The Meconopsis Group, to sort out the perceived confusion in the identities and names of the big perennial blue poppies in cultivation.

John Mitchell of the Royal Botanic Garden was largely instrumental in the invaluable involvement and encouragement of the Royal Botanic Garden Edinburgh. I have always also felt grateful to all the *Meconopsis* enthusiasts who joined The Meconopsis Group, donated plants for the identification and naming trial and have loyally supported our work. I greatly valued the help of our management committee over many years, in particular our efficient secretary, Norma McDowall, and treasurer, Peggy Anderson. Christopher Brickell kindly advised us on how to set about sorting out the plethora of plants we were presented with. The late Cameron Carmichael suggested registering my ever-increasing collection of big blue poppies as a Plant Heritage National Collection. Without the expertise, hard work and dedication of my friend Peter Taylor, I do not think we would have been able to get our web site launched so successfully. The role of specialist nursery owners Beryl McNaughton and Ian Christie in enthusiastically promoting the named cultivars is greatly appreciated. This also applies to Jim Jermyn who started the Group's successful seed exchange and helped in negotiations that led to The Royal Horticultural Society undertaking the trial of big blue poppies for the Award of Garden Merit at Harlow Carr. The RHS's role on taking on this commitment is also greatly appreciated. In more recent years. I have greatly appreciated the support, encouragement and help of Pat Murphy of Holehird Garden in Windermere for her whole-hearted enthusiasm for the big blue poppies and other members of the genus *Meconopsis*.

It has been a pleasure to work with both Pat Lewis who did the book layout and design, and Nigel Mitchell of Biddles who arranged the printing; both worked very efficiently to tight time schedules. Pat liaised with all four members of the family and Nigel offered many helpful suggestions which we adopted.

But most of all I am grateful to my husband, Lewis, and our two daughters, Catherine and Rowena for their encouragement and help in making this book come to fruition: this would not have happened but for their involvement. Catherine with her artistic and horticultural skills, assisted greatly in choosing which photographs to use amongst the plethora available. Also essential were Lewis and Rowena's inputs with their scientific writing and publishing skills and knowledge.

Picture credits

I am grateful to: Jim Smith for the cover photograph of *M.* 'Jimmy Bayne' and for the close-up studio photographs of *Meconopsis* 'Lingholm' fruit capsules and seeds, Bob Mitchell for the historic photographs of *M. grandis* in the Sherriff's garden at Ascreavie in 1975 and of *M. grandis* 'Branklyn' at the Savill Garden in 1996, to Pat Murphy for the photographs of the yet to be formally named fine purple form of *M.* 'Lingholm' at Branklyn Garden and to Steve McNamara for the correct cream-coloured photograph of *M. x sarsonsii* also at Branklyn Garden.

Contents

Introduction

At the end of the twentieth century it had become apparent to a few gardeners in Scotland that there existed much confusion in the identities and naming of the range of beautiful garden forms (cultivars) of the plants now known as the Big Perennial Blue Poppies. This term embraces three species of the genus *Meconopsis* and a number of hybrids of garden origin derived from them. The big blue poppies are characterised by having clusters of large flowers (10–15 cm plus in diameter) with four petals, a prominent boss of golden anthers and a prominent style, concentrated near the apex of the flowering stem which is generally around 1–1.5 m or more in height at flowering. The leaves occur both as basal rosettes, and also at intervals up the flowering stem. Given the right garden conditions, they are perennial, persisting year after year. They can make a fine display flowering from late spring to mid-summer.

My interest in *Meconopsis* began in the late 1970s when I began growing these plants in my garden in Dunblane in central Scotland. I started with *M. baileyi*, but then a builder friend, Jimmy Bayne, offered me what he called a "better" one, but with no name, that he had found while excavating for a garage in Dunblane twenty years before. Experts could not name it when seeing it at a *Meconopsis* workshop at The Royal Botanic Gardens Edinburgh a few years later. They agreed that it was sufficiently distinct and valuable that it should be given a name. Eventually I published a full description of it in "The Rock Garden", the journal of the Scottish Rock Garden Club, naming it *Meconopsis* 'Jimmy Bayne'. That led to my becoming involved in studying *Meconopsis* in greater detail.

In 1998, together with nurseryman, Mervyn Kessell, I founded The Meconopsis Group, with the support of the Royal Botanic Gardens Edinburgh. The primary aim of The Meconopsis Group — which comprises gardeners and horticulturists with a particular interest in the genus — is to clarify the identities and names of the big perennial blue poppies in cultivation. Most of these are hybrids of garden origin. Since its founding, The Meconopsis Group has characterised most of the big blue poppies found to be in cultivation, largely in Scotland, but also in the north of England, Ireland and a few locations elsewhere. This book includes the results of our investigations and hopefully will inspire further work into this genus, including both the large number of *Meconopsis* species and some other hybrids.

The process of study has been to collect as many donations of big blue poppies as possible from Meconopsis enthusiasts. These have then been grown as far as possible, like with like, in trial beds. They have then been observed and assessed over a number of years (often over more than 15 years) by a group of people who have wide experience with these plants. Decisions on identities and any new names have then been presented to members of The Meconopsis Group at group meetings for agreement and ratification.

Species in garden cultivation

Undoubtedly the two species most relevant to the origin of the garden forms described in this book are the perennial and taller, blue-flowered species, namely *Meconopsis grandis* and *Meconopsis baileyi*. Another tall blue-flowered species, *Meconopsis simplicifolia*, is also thought to have contributed to the origin of some of the garden forms and it is speculated that yet other species with different colours of flowers may also have played a part.

Meconopsis grandis subspecies *grandis* was introduced into cultivation in about 1896 and there are photographs in the archives at the Royal Botanic Garden Edinburgh showing it growing well there in 1906. An important later introduction of *M. grandis* was from Eastern Bhutan by George Sherriff in 1934. This eastern form is now recognised as the subspecies *orientalis*.

Meconopsis baileyi, the other most significant big blue poppy species for the purposes of this book, was discovered by Col. F.M. Bailey in south-eastern Tibet in 1913 and then introduced into cultivation as seeds by Frank Kingdon Ward in 1924. This introduction was very successful and it became the most widely grown of the big blue poppy species. George Taylor re-classified it as *M. betonicifolia* in 1934, the name by which it was well known until 2010 when Christopher Grey-Wilson showed that its original circumscription as *M. baileyi* was the correct one. *M betonicifolia* is a distinct, although closely related, species native to north-west China, and has not yet been introduced into cultivation.

M. simplicifolia has been introduced on a number of occasions from 1848 onwards into the 20th century. There was a time when it was quite widely grown, but this no longer seems to be so. At present it is a rarity, but it is hoped that soon it may be reintroduced.

Hybrids in garden cultivation

Although it is not well documented, it is apparent that when these three species, — namely, *M baileyi*, *M grandis* subsp *grandis* and subsp *orientalis* and *M. simplicifolia* — and possibly others, were introduced from their geographically widely separated wild habitats into the close confines of gardens, they were cross-pollinated by visiting insects. This undeniably resulted in a range of hybrids, many of which were sterile. Although much of this hybridisation occurred without human intervention, on occasion gardeners were responsible; here again the reporting is scanty. The outcome of this uncontrolled hybridisation and lack of recording was the confused situation that led to the founding of The Meconopsis Group.

Because sterile hybrids do not set viable seed, the only way to produce more plants is vegetatively by lifting and dividing whole plants or by removing rooted pieces from the edges of such plants (unless micropropagation also becomes feasible in future). This means that every division is genetically identical to its "parent" and therefore its identification is not compromised by the variation to be expected in seedlings (unless the taxon in question has undergone a long and rigorous process of selection by nurserymen; this is the norm with many commercially available cultivars of garden plants, but not, as yet, with *Meconopsis*.)

The sterility of most of the big blue poppies means that it should be possible to characterise and name the range of hybrids to be found growing in gardens. Based on this understanding, The Meconopsis Group embarked on this project to characterise and name these cultivars.

At the start of the process of sorting out the identities and nomenclature for the big perennial blue poppies there were various problems concerning the many hybrid samples donated to the assessment trial. Some plants came with no name, others, obviously identical, were received under two different names and others came with invalid names. In order to help clarify the identities of the hybrids three Groups were established, based on certain characteristics, as follows:

(i)   George Sherriff Group: plants considered to be clones derived from *M. grandis* seed collected by George Sherriff in Bhutan in 1934 with the collector's number GS600
(ii) Infertile Blue Group: sterile cultivars other than those belonging to the previous Group
(iii) Fertile Blue Group: fertile hybrids; these plants are probably fertile as a result of chromosome doubling.

In addition to the cultivars there are the three species that are grown in gardens (namely *M. grandis, M. baileyi* and *M. simplicifolia)* and several cultivars which appear to have a close affinity to the three species; these are placed in a separate category in this book, Species and aff. Species. Also, a few cultivars have white petals and are therefore easily distinguished from the blue forms and have been placed separately in a fifth category: White Forms.

Although these groupings are now less important, in this book the plants in each group are described together as it is easier to compare similar looking plants on adjacent pages. The features of each of the five groups are described at the beginning of each section. Largely, within the sections the descriptions of each cultivar are arranged alphabetically. All species and hybrids are listed in the Index.

Characteristic features of the big perennial blue poppies

The various stages of development are all attractive features of these plants — all, that is, except perhaps for the dead flower stems in late summer and when the resting buds are out of sight, underground, in the winter! The big perennial blue poppies are all herbaceous perennials. This means that they are made up of annual stems, leaves and flowers that grow each year from perennial roots. Over winter the plants persist as resting buds just under the soil until the following spring.

The appearance of the various parts of the plants during development, starting with the emergence of young leaves in spring, help greatly in cultivar recognition. This is so, even though the initial rosette of basal leaves, the flowering stem with its cauline leaves, the flowers and the second set of basal leaves that develop after flowering, are often quite variable. However, despite this variation there is no doubt about the integrity and distinctiveness of each of the cultivars. The aim of this book is to illustrate for each species or cultivar its characteristic features.

Plant Awards

The merits of these plants for garden cultivation have been assessed in two trials. The first was carried out at the Royal Botanic Garden Edinburgh and at the author's garden in Central Scotland by the Joint Rock Garden Plant Committee (JRGPC). The JRGPC assigns the following awards: Preliminary Commendation (PC), Award of Merit (AM) and First Class Certificate (FCC). The second was an extensive three-year trial performed at Harlow Carr, Yorkshire by the Royal Horticultural Society (RHS) for the Award of Garden Merit (AGM). A number of these plants have been awarded an AGM, while others were considered "near-misses". Details of the highest award each cultivar has received are indicated in the individual entries for the cultivar.

Plant Descriptions

In the following section each of the species and hybrids in cultivation is described under the headings listed below.

Name: The plant's full name is given and if it has received an award then its highest award is shown, i.e. Award of Garden Merit (AGM), First Class Certificate (FCC), Award of Merit (AM) and Preliminary Commendation (PC).

The following symbols are also used:

† indicates: not yet ratified by The Meconopsis Group, or submitted to the International Cultivar Registration Authority for validation and establishment of the name

Δ indicates: "near miss" for an Award of Garden Merit in the 2010–2013 RHS trial

Ψ is used to show those cultivars which are usually infertile but that sometimes set seed.

N.B. Many of the cultivars listed as sterile, do, in fact, often produce a few, sometimes many, apparently well-developed seeds. These may or may not germinate readily to produce new plants. Unless, or until, it is established by stringent trials over several generations that any such plants "breed true", it is important that any seedlings from named cultivars are not given the parents' cultivar names, but are labelled for example, ex 'Blue Butterfly', ex 'Dippoolbank', ex 'Willie Duncan' etc. This reservation does not apply to 'Lingholm' or plants from the Fertile Blue Group.

Background: The origins of the cultivars, if known, are given. The group in which it has been placed is shown as George Sherriff Group (GSG), Infertile Blue Group (IBG), Fertile Blue Group (FBG), White Form (WF) or species or aff. species (Sp). The unique identifying number for each cultivar, The Meconopsis Group (MG) number, is also given.

Notable features: The appearance of the plant including its flower, leaves and fruit capsule.

Flowering season: Whether early, mid-season or late. Which month this corresponds to varies from year to year but may range from late April to mid-July.

Compare: Other cultivars that are similar in overall appearance or in specific aspects.

Availability and cultivation: Whether generally available in garden centres, specialist nurseries, seed exchanges or rare is noted, as is how easy the species or hybrid is to grow and by what means it is propagated assuming the conditions for cultivation are suitable. A list of nurseries and advice on cultivation are given in sections at the end of the book.

Photographs: Photographs in the following pages showing different aspects of the plants are not to scale.

SECTION A: Species and aff. ("near") Species

Background: This first section encompasses the species of big perennial blue poppies in cultivation, together with some that are deemed to be either conspecific with one these species or very closely related to them. The undoubted species are *M. baileyi* and *M. grandis.* Their relationship to the subspecies and cultivars are shown below.

Figure 1: The relationship between the species, *M. baileyi* and *M. grandis,* and subspecies (ssp.) and cultivars (cv.).

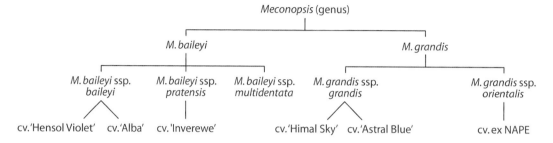

The taxa included here as aff. (affinity) species are *M.* 'Strathspey' and 'Great Glen'. Both were received into the identification and naming trial as *M. grandis* and possess features very similar to those of the species, but as they are sterile or very near sterile they are regarded as garden-originated hybrids. A third big perennial blue poppy species is *M. simplicifolia.* Once commonly grown in gardens, it appears to be a very rare plant in cultivation at the present time.

Photographs: *M. baileyi (top left), M. grandis ssp. grandis* 'Himal Sky' *(top right),*
M. grandis ssp. grandis 'Astral Blue' *(bottom left), M. grandis orientalis* ex NAPE *(bottom right).*

1 *Meconopsis baileyi* (AGM) and *Meconopsis baileyi* 'Alba'

Background: *Meconopsis baileyi* is probably the most well known and most widely grown of the big perennial blue poppies, introduced from seed collected in south-eastern Tibet by Frank Kingdon Ward where the western traveller, Colonel F.M. Bailey, had discovered it in 1913. *Sp., MG39* (*M. baileyi*) and *MG40* (*M. baileyi* 'Alba'). *Notable features:* Usually raised from seed, each plant is an individual with its own distinct genetic make-up and thus there is some variability. *Flowers:* Normally varying shades of blue, also a pure white form, *M. baileyi* 'Alba'. Several flowers (8–10cm diameter) arise from the false whorl at the top of the flowering stem, while further flowers, one per leaf axil, arise below this. *Emerging leaves:* Broadly elliptical, heart-shaped at the base of the lamina. *Mature leaves:* Broadly elliptical, cordate at the base of the lamina and sub-obtuse at the apex. *Fruit capsule:* Ovoid body, densely clothed with short

bristles, style and stigma short. *Flowering season:* generally late. *Compare:* *M. baileyi* ssp. *pratensis,* 'Inverewe' and *M. baileyi* 'Hensol Violet'. *Availability and cultivation:* Widely available from garden centres, nurseries, and seed companies; fertile, readily raised from seed and by division. One of the easiest to grow.

2 *Meconopsis baileyi* ssp. *multidentata* (Grey-Wilson, nova sp (2014))

Background: *Meconopsis baileyi* ssp *multidentata* was introduced as seed by Michael Wickenden of Cally Gardens in 2003 from Arunachal Pradesh, near the Myanmar border. Plants were raised and distributed. *Sp., MG109.* **Notable features:** *V*ery like *M. baileyi* ssp. *pratensis*, but differs in several respects including relatively longer basal leaves and lateral-facing flowers (Grey-Wilson, 2014). **Flowering period:** Early-mid season. **Compare:** *M. baileyi* ssp. *pratensis*, 'Inverewe', *baileyi* sp. *baileyi*. **Availability and cultivation:** Unavailable at present; difficult to cultivate.

3 *Meconopsis baileyi* 'Hensol Violet'

Background: *M. baileyi* 'Hensol Violet' was raised by Lady Catherine Henderson, at Hensol Castle in Dumfriesshire towards the end of the twentieth century. It was recognised as distinct and then given its cultivar name. *Sp. MG41.* ***Notable features:*** Very similar to *M. baileyi* except for its striking violet- purple flower. ***Flowering period:*** Late-mid season, ahead of *M. baileyi.* ***Compare:*** *M. baileyi.* ***Availability and cultivation:*** Specialist nurseries and seedsmen's catalogues. Fertile and comes true from seed. Readily propagated by division.

4 *Meconopsis baileyi* ssp. *pratensis*

Background: This sub-species of *baileyi* was raised from seed and introduced by Frank Kingdon Ward, probably in 1926. It has persisted in cultivation in small numbers ever since. It closely resembles *M.* 'Inverewe' so much so that the general consensus now is that it may be identical to 'Inverewe', although it appears much more difficult to grow than the latter. *Sp., MG42.* ***Notable features:*** Appearance very similar to that of 'Inverewe' although it is taller and much more difficult to propagate. It can only be easily distinguished by close comparison with 'Inverewe' growing in the same garden. ***Flowering season:*** Mid to late season, but ahead of *M. baileyi*. ***Compare:*** *M.* 'Inverewe' and *M. baileyi*. ***Availability and cultivation:*** Rare at present; sterile, does not form abundant off-sets.

5 *Meconopsis* 'Inverewe' (AGM)

Background: Sterile plant grown for many years at Inverewe Gardens, Wester Ross as *betonicilfolia* (now *baileyi*). The Meconopsis Group was asked to clarify its identity. Named *M.* 'Inverewe' in 2007, but since then perceived to be conspecific with *baileyi* ssp.*pratensis* (Grey-Wilson 2014). *IBG*ᵠ, *MG18*. ***Notable features:*** *Flowers:* Sky-blue, nodding due to sharp deflection of the pedicels close to their proximal ends. A two-tier effect often results from the lengthening of the pedicel of the first flower to open, ahead of a second group within a false whorl, thus forming a second, lower tier. *Emerging leaves:* Intense suffusion with red-purple pigment with bases of the leaf blades cordate or truncate. *Fruit capsule:* To all intents and purposes sterile, unlike fully fertile *baileyi*, similar ovoid body, covered densely with short bristles; style short and stigma rounded and prominent. ***Flowering season:*** Mid-season, ahead of *M. baileyi*.

Compare: *M. baileyi* ssp. *pratensis*, *M. baileyi*.

Availability and cultivation: Specialist nurseries; easily propagated by division.

15

6 *Meconopsis grandis* ssp. *grandis* 'Himal Sky' (AGM)

Background: *Meconopsis grandis* growing in the wild and in cultivation is very variable. 'Himal Sky' is a cultivar within one of three subspecies in cultivation. *Sp., MG27.* **Notable features:** *Flowers:* A single flower arises from the false whorl at the apex of a short flowering stem. Flowers are blue or blue-mauve, normally with four, but sometimes with 5 or 6 ovate, wavy petals. *Emerging and mature leaves:* narrowly elliptical, virtually devoid of teeth on the margins of the leaf blades, and devoid of red-purple pigmentation. *Fruit capsule:* Large, glabrous body maturing at the apex of a greatly lengthened pedicel and filled with large viable seeds that breed true to form, style short and broad, stigma prominent. **Flowering season:** Often the earliest. **Compare:** 'Astral Blue', 'Great Glen', 'Kingsbarns'. **Availability and cultivation:** Specialist nurseries and specialist society seed exchanges; long-lived and is readily increased by division, breeds true from seed.

7 *Meconopsis grandis* ssp. *grandis* 'Astral Blue'

Background: *Meconopsis grandis* growing in the wild and in cultivation is very variable. 'Astral Blue' is a cultivar within one of three subspecies in cultivation. *Sp., MG28*. *Notable features:* Some features are similar to the cultivar 'Himal Sky', others are quite distinct. *Flowers:* Always bears a single flower within the false whorl at the apex of a short flowering stem. After the flowers open, the pedicels lengthen greatly during fruit capsules maturation. Flowers deep blue, sometimes 5 or 6 petals, petals are broadly ovate and over-lapping. *Emerging leaves:* Slightly suffused with red-purple pigment. *Mature leaves:* Narrow and elliptical, but broader than in 'Himal Sky', possessing a few well-defined, dentate teeth on the margins. *Fruit capsule*: Large, glabrous, with viable seeds. *Flowering period:* Mid-season, significantly later than 'Himal Sky'. *Compare:* 'Himal Sky', 'Strathspey' and 'Great Glen'. *Availability and cultivation:* Specialist nurseries and specialist society seed exchanges; fertile, grown from seed or by division.

8 *Meconopsis grandis* ssp. *grandis* - Sikkim form and others

Three subspecies of *M. grandis* have been recognised, *M. grandis* ssp. *jumlaensis* in west Nepal, *M. grandis* ssp. *grandis* growing mainly around eastern Nepal, and *M. grandis* ssp. *orientalis* growing far to the east in Bhutan and Arunachal Pradesh (Grey-Wilson 2014). Of these, *M. grandis* spp. *grandis* has been growing in the gardens of a number of *Meconopsis* enthusiasts in the UK for many years, whereas ssp. *orientalis* has now just got a toe-hold in cultivation, and ssp. jumlaensis is not in cultivation. Some forms of *grandis* ssp. *grandis,* derived from wild collections of seeds many decades ago, acquired the names "Sikkim form" and "early Sikkim form". It is not clear if these names are justified and how they differ from each other, nor how they differ from any other forms of *grandis* ssp. *grandis* in cultivation. At the present time some are fertile and some are sterile. The photographs here are examples from three different gardens with the purported "Sikkim" or "early Sikkim form" of *grandis* ssp. *grandis* and illustrate the differences. Bottom right is a photograph taken by Bob Mitchell of "Sikkim form" identified for him by Betty Sherriff in her garden at Ascreavie in 1975. The other two are photographs of plants of alleged *grandis* 'Sikkim' form taken much more recently by two other *Meconopsis* experts.

9 *Meconopsis grandis* ssp. *orientalis* ex NAPE

Background: *M. grandis* growing in the wild and in cultivation is very variable. Currently there are three recognised subspecies, namely: *grandis* ssp. *grandis*, *grandis* ssp. *orientalis*, and *grandis* subsp. *jumlaensis*. *M. grandis* ssp *orientalis* is native to areas far to the east, in eastern Bhutan and western Arunachal Pradesh, the general area from which George Sherriff collected *M. grandis* GS600 seed in 1934. *M. grandis* ssp *orientalis* is believed to be the progenitor of the sterile George Sherriff Group of cultivars in cultivation. At the present time ssp. *orientalis* has just a toe-hold in cultivation as seed was introduced to Scotland from the Nagaland Arunachal Pradesh Expedition (NAPE) in 2003. *Sp, MG32.*

10 *Meconopsis* 'Great Glen'

Background: This plant was donated for the trial as "*M. grandis* early Sikkim form" by Mike and Polly Stone, Fort Augustus in 1998. The large promising-looking fruit-capsules are intrinsically sterile, although a few well-developed seeds are occasionally found. It is not known if the seeds are viable or come true. The name was ratified by The Meconopsis Group in 2012. *Sp., MG31.* ***Notable features:*** *Flowers:* Exceptionally large, sky-blue with broadly ovate, overlapping petals. *Emerging leaves:* Petioles become lengthened such that leaves bend over towards the ground. False whorl leaves mostly are large. *Mature leaves:* New leaves after flowering are unusually large, broadly elliptic with a few dentate teeth on the margins of the leaf blades. *Fruit capsule:* Exceptionally large body, knobbly with substantial bristles, twisted style and stout stigma. Pedicels greatly lengthened after flowering. ***Flowering season:*** Very early. ***Compare:*** Other *grandis* forms, e.g. 'Himal Sky', 'Astral Blue' 'Strathspey'. ***Availability and cultivation:*** Specialist nurseries; readily propagated by division.

11 *Meconopsis* 'Strathspey' (PC)^Δ

Background: Purchased from Jack Drake's nursery by James Gauld as *M. grandis* collected in west Nepal by Polunin, Sykes and Williams. At some stage it became sterile possibly through hybridisation. Because of its stated origin and morphological similarity to the species, it is placed here under *Sp., MG30*.
Notable features: *Flowers:* Strikingly upright with one to three, deep purple-blue, lateral-facing cup-shaped flowers arising from a false whorl of several large leaves at the apex of the flower stem. The pedicels lengthen quite markedly so that the flowers "sail" above the foliage. The petals are somewhat pleated, ovate and broadly over-lapping. *Emerging leaves:* Ascending, oblong-elliptic, slightly red-purple pigmented and with the margin indented with neat serrate teeth. *Mature leaves:* Similar in shape, but with no red-purple pigment. *Fruit capsules:* densely clothed with spreading bristles. **Flowering season:** Early. **Compare:** Other forms of *M. grandis*. **Availability and cultivation:** Specialist nurseries; readily propagated by division.

Section B: *Meconopsis* George Sherriff Group

There are about 30 clones of big perennial blue poppies thriving in gardens that fit within the parameters established for the George Sherriff Group. This Group was established by The Meconopsis Group to accommodate the different sterile plants previously known collectively by the name *M. grandis* GS600. GS600 is the collector's number for seed collected by George Sherriff from an expedition in 1934 to eastern Bhutan. The collector's name and number "*M. grandis* GS600" should only be used if plants are derived from the original collected seed, or plants derived from them by division. This is very unlikely for the many plants that were being called *grandis* GS600 seventy years later at the end of the twentieth century. A number of clones have been selected and given cultivar names, and the names of some others have yet to be ratified by The Meconopsis Group. Our observations convince us that many of these sterile "*grandis* GS600" cultivars, although very similar to one another, are distinct. Illustrated on this page are some cultivars that are very similar to one another and some that are very different. Interestingly, there are some recent reports of some of the cultivars producing reasonable amounts of viable seed – intriguing, but as yet unexplained – investigations needed!

Top row, from left to right: M. 'Ascreavie',
M. 'Susan's Reward', M. 'Jimmy Bayne'
Bottom left: M. 'Barney's Blue'
Bottom right: M. 'Huntfield'

12 *Meconopsis 'Ascreavie' (PC)*[Δ]

Background: Widely grown, the name 'Ascreavie' after George Sherriff's
garden in Angus, was ratified by The Meconopsis Group in 2001. *GSG, MG5*.
Notable features: *Flowers*: Blue, often with a mauve or purplish cast, narrow
wavy petals giving a "windmill effect", quite distinct from the majority of GSG
cultivars; flowering stem often leaning. *Emerging leaves*: Intensely suffused
with a red-purple pigment, relatively broad, clothed densely with short hairs.
Very soon after emergence, leaves become noticeably spreading. *Mature leaves*:
Leaf blades with deeply serrate teeth on the margins, tips mostly acute. *Fruit
capsule*: Relatively narrow ellipsoid body, furnished with short, densely-packed
bristles over the whole surface, including the sutures between the carpels, style
noticeably longer than in the "bowl-shaped" GSG cultivars. *Flowering season*:
Late. *Compare*: 'Inverleith', 'Sue Barnes'. *Availability and cultivation*: Specialist
nurseries; sterile, readily propagated by division

23

13 *Meconopsis* 'Barney's Blue' (AM)^Δ

Background: 'Barney's Blue' came to light in 2000 in the garden George and Betty Sherriff created at Ascreavie House, Kingoldrum, Angus, now owned by Barney Baron after whom the plant was named. Probably not raised by the Sherriffs, but acquired after they retired from India in 1949. *GSG, MG12.* **Notable features:** *Flowers:* Unusual, colour changing from bud opening to maturity, from the centre outwards from deep magenta to mauvy-blue to a final clear blue, giving a tri-coloured effect to a clump. *Emerging leaves:* A little later emerging than other GSG cultivars and lack the usual intense red-purple pigmentation. *Mature leaves:* Paleish green. *Fruit capsule:* Typical for GSG, densely covered with short, pale-coloured bristles. **Flowering season:** Late. **Compare:** Other GSG cultivars. **Availability and cultivation:** Specialist nurseries; sterile but readily increased by division.

14 *Meconopsis* 'Branklyn' (was awarded FCC)

Background: In 1963 the Royal Horticultural Society awarded a First Class Certificate to a plant of *Meconopsis grandis* GS600 submitted to a show in London. Jack Drake at Inshriach Nursery had raised it from seed probably sent to him from the Rentons of Branklyn Garden and it was subsequently named *M. grandis* 'Branklyn'. In 1966 *Meconopsis* 'Branklyn' was photographed by Bob Mitchell growing well in the Savill Garden at Windsor but subsequently it was lost from there. It was also lost from Branklyn Garden, after its introduction there. Since that time it has not been possible to identify unequivocally plants that are propagules of the original 'Branklyn' amongst a number of purported replacements. M. 'Branklyn' was clearly a round-petalled GSG clone, with ovate petals, but which, if any, of those still extant that have been submitted to The Meconopsis Group as 'Branklyn', is the correct one? The Plant Finder lists 'Branklyn' as "ambiguous". Two photographs on this page are of collections of purported specimens of 'Branklyn' planted in the last few years at Branklyn Garden in Perth (*left*), and in my own garden (*top right*), together with Bob Mitchell's 1966 photograph (*bottom right*).

15 *Meconopsis* 'Dalemain' (AGM)

Background: M 'Dalemain', grows in several large beds in a woodland setting at Dalemain Garden in Cumbria. *GSG, MG2*. *Notable features:* Very similar to 'Huntfield', 'Susan's Reward', 'Jimmy Bayne' and other GSG clones. Named at the owner's request as "their blue poppy" as the garden is open to visitors. *Flowers:* Shallow bowl-shaped with ovate, broadly over-lapping petals varying in colour from a pure blue to mauve-blue to even purple on occasion. This applies to the various flowers on a given plant in a given year, from year to year, and to plants in different parts of the same garden. *Emerging leaves:* Broadly elliptic, suffused with a red-purple pigment. *Mature leaves:* Broadly elliptic, margins indented with dentate/serrate teeth, resulting in a handsome leafy plant. *Fruit capsule:* Narrowly ellipsoid body, clothed densely with short fawn-coloured bristles. *Flowering season:* Late. *Compare:* 'Huntfield', 'Susan's Reward' and 'Jimmy Bayne'. *Availability and cultivation:* Specialist nurseries; sterile, propagated readily by division.

16 *Meconopsis* 'Huntfield' (AM)^Δ

Background: Purchased by Allan Jamieson at Huntfield House in the Scottish Borders. The cultivar name was approved in 2002. A "near-miss" in the AGM trial. *GSG, MG4.* ***Notable features:*** Very similar to 'Dalemain', 'Susan's Reward', 'Jimmy Bayne' and other GSG clones. It appears to produce particularly abundant numbers of off-sets, making it a good nurseryman's plant! *Flowers:* Ovate, rounded, broadly over-lapping petals. Colour may vary (ranging from blue through to purple) for reasons that are as yet unclear – scientific research is needed! *Emerging leaves:* Broadly elliptic with suffusion of red-purple pigment. *Mature leaves:* Broadly elliptic, resulting in a handsome leafy plant. *Fruit capsule:* Narrowly ellipsoid body, clothed densely with short bristles. ***Flowering season:*** Late. ***Compare:*** 'Dalemain', 'Jimmy Bayne', 'Susan's Reward' and others. ***Availability and cultivation:*** Specialist nurseries; sterile, readily propagated from the generous number of off-sets.

17 *Meconopsis* 'Inverleith'

Background: Grown in the Woodland Garden at the Royal Botanic Garden Edinburgh with a label stating it to be *M. grandis* GS600 with accession number 1965 1278, although not given a cultivar name until The Meconopsis Group decided on 'Inverleith' in 2009. It would appear to be the original *M. grandis* GS600, but there is uncertainty about its history before 1965 and also it does not set fertile seed. *GSG, MG6. Notable features:* Many features like 'Ascreavie'. *Flowers:* Blue with 'wind-mill' arrangement of petals separated and rather narrow and frilly. *Emerging leaves:* Intense suffusion of red-purple pigment. *Mature leaves:* Rather twisted leaf blades with serrate marginal teeth hooked at the tips and are more deeply incised than in 'Ascreavie'. *Fruit capsule:* Like those of 'Ascreavie', but in a slightly more extreme form, i.e. a narrower capsule body and a longer style. *Flowering season:* Late. *Compare: M.* 'Ascreavie', 'Sue Barnes' and 'John Lawson'. *Availability and cultivation:* Specialist nurseries; readily propagated by division.

18 *Meconopsis* 'Jimmy Bayne' (AM)^Δ

Background: Found growing in Dunblane, central Scotland, in about 1962 by Jimmy Bayne and given to the author in about 1980. Establishing its name led directly to the founding of The Meconopsis Group in 1998. A "near-miss" in the AGM trial. *GSG, MG1*. *Notable features:* Very similar to 'Dalemain', 'Susan's Reward', and 'Huntfield', but a little more elegant and less robust-looking. *Flowers:* Ovate, rounded, broadly overlapping petals, either pure blue or blue tinged with mauve. *Emerging leaves:* Broad, suffused with a red-purple pigment and covered densely with short hairs. *Mature leaves:* Broadly elliptic resulting in a handsome leafy plant. The leaves are slightly more rounded at the apex than in other GSG cultivars, and the teeth on the margins are more regular. *Fruit capsule:* Ellipsoid body, clothed densely with short bristles, style moderately long and stigma moderately prominent. *Flowering season:* Late season. *Compare:* 'Dalemain', 'Huntfield', 'Susan's Reward' and others. *Availability and cultivation:* Specialist nurseries; sterile, readily propagated by division.

19 *Meconopsis* 'John Lawson'†

Background: Jack Drake established the well-known Inshriach Nursery at Aviemore in 1938. John Lawson, his successor donated this cultivar to the identification trial and it was later named after him. *GSG, MG94.* **Notable features:** Similar to 'Ascreavie', the most significant difference being that it is a shorter, smaller plant. *Flowers:* One of the GSG "wind-mill" type cultivars with narrow wavy petals; varies in colour, sometimes blue, sometimes more purple than blue. *Emerging leaves:* Intensely suffused with red-purple pigment, relatively broad, clothed densely with short hairs. *Mature leaves:* Margins of the leaf blades indented with deeply serrate teeth, the tips mostly acute. *Fruit capsule:* Relatively narrow ellipsoid body furnished densely with short bristles, style noticeably longer than in the "bowl-shaped" GSG cultivars. **Flowering season:** Late. **Compare:** 'Ascreavie', 'Inverleith', and 'Sue Barnes'. **Availability and cultivation:** Rare; propagated by division.

20 *Meconopsis* 'Springhill'†

Background: At one time this member of George Sherriff Group was growing in large beds at Logan Botanic Garden in south-western Scotland, but it appears to have become rare. The name is "tentatively accepted" in RHS's Plant Finder. *GSG, MG80.* ***Notable features:*** Very similar to such round-petalled forms of GSG such as 'Jimmy Bayne', 'Huntfield', 'Dalemain' and 'Susan's Reward', but with certain exceptions. Leaf emergence and flowering are a little later. Also it is a little shorter at flowering and there are fewer teeth (normally only 4 or 5) on the margins of each side of the leaf blades. ***Flowering season:*** Late. ***Compare:*** ' Huntfield', 'Jimmy Bayne', 'Susan's Reward' and 'Dalemain'. ***Availability and cultivation:*** Rare; sterile, readily propagated by division.

21 *Meconopsis* 'Sue Barnes'[†]

Background: Donated by Sue Barnes of Biggar Park in the Scottish Borders, for study by The Meconopsis Group. Sue Barnes was given it by Sylvia McCosh, former owner of Dalemain, Cumbria and Huntfield House in the Scottish Borders. It is clearly a GSG clone of the "wind-mill" type, but has one distinct difference from others in the Group. *GSG, MG73.*
Notable features: Similar to 'Ascreavie', the most significant difference being that the young emerging leaves lack the suffusion of intense red-purple pigment. *Flowers*: Blue, of the "wind-mill" type, with wavy, not overlapping petals. *Emerging leaves*: Notably little suffusion of red-purple pigment, relatively broad, clothed densely with short hairs. *Mature leaves:* Leaf blade margins serrate, tips mostly sub-acute. *Fruit capsule*: Narrow ellipsoid capsule body furnished densely with short bristles; style long. *Flowering season:* Late. *Compare:* 'Ascreavie', 'Inverleith'. *Availability and cultivation:* Rare at present; readily propagated by division.

22 *Meconopsis* 'Susan's Reward' (AGM)

Background: Sue Sym seen here in her garden in Edinburgh with some of her newly divided poppies was given this by Betty Sherriff in 1972 after she had spent time helping Betty at Ascreavie. It was named by The Meconopsis Group in 2008 and is one of four similar named GSG clones. (The others are 'Huntfield', 'Jimmy Bayne' and 'Dalemain'.) This plant was selected for naming because of its reputation for performing particularly well in areas with a drier climate. *GSG, MG3*. **Notable features:** *Flowers:* Deep blue, tinged with purple, one of the round-petalled forms of GSG clones, having flowers with ovate, broadly overlapping petals. *Emerging leaves:* Possess suffusion of red-purple

pigment. and covered densely with short hairs. *Mature leaves:* Both the basal and stem leaves are broadly elliptic resulting in a handsome leafy plant. *Fruit capsule: Body* ellipsoid, clothed densely with short bristles, style moderately short, stigma moderately prominent. **Flowering season:** Late. **Compare:** 'Huntfield', 'Jimmy Bayne', 'Dalemain'. ***Availability and cultivation:*** Specialist nurseries; sterile, readily propagated by division.

Section C: *Meconopsis* Infertile Blue Group

This Group is much more disparate than the George Sherriff Group as it includes all the infertile hybrids not considered to be within the George Sherriff Group. It also excludes the white petalled hybrids that are considered separately.

The most important feature of the Infertile Blue Group is that these hybrid cultivars are by and large sterile and do not produce fruit capsules filled with viable seeds. This is in contrast to the species and the now well-known fully fertile cultivar 'Lingholm' (Fertile Blue Group), both of which reliably produce fruit capsules filled with viable seeds. Some members of Infertile Blue Group do, in fact, regularly produce a limited number of viable seeds; others only occasionally do so, but do not produce fruit capsules filled to the capacity expected if fully fertile. Several contrasting members of Infertile Blue Group are illustrated on this page.

Photographs on this page and opposite:
1) *M.* 'Houndwood'
2) *M.* 'Cameron Carmichael'
3) *M.* 'James Aitken'
4) *M.* 'Ardcuil'
5) *M.* 'Slieve Donard'
6) *M.* 'Mrs Jebb'
7) *M.* 'Blue Butterfly'
8) *M.* 'Evelyn'

23 *Meconopsis* 'Ardcuil'†

Background: Three plants donated for the naming trial from three different donors proved to be the same cultivar. Two came labelled as *M. grandis* GS600, though clearly not so. This unusual cultivar was named 'Ardcuil', the home of the presumed decades-ago early grower of this clone, Major-General Murray-Lyon. *IBG, MG50. Notable features:* Very late emergence of the leaves and very late flowering. *Flowers:* Flowers ovate, with smooth-edged petals slightly overlapping. Petals tend to be retained until after the fruit capsules have become vertical. *Emerging leaves:* Distinctive rosettes of small, firm, ascending, broadly ovate leaves. *Mature leaves:* Petioles lengthen greatly, leaf blades broadly oblong-elliptic, margins with a few shallow teeth, tips sub-obtuse. *Fruit capsule:* Narrowly ellipsoid body clothed densely with short bristles, the styles straight-sided and long, the stigmas round and prominent. *Flowering season:* Late, often the latest. *Compare:* None. *Availability and cultivation:* Not available at present; sterile, propagation by division, best carried out when new growth is beginning in spring.

24 *Meconopsis* 'Bobby Masterton' (AGM)

Background: The Meconopsis Group named this in 2003 after Bobby Masterton, who created the exceptional Cluny Garden, Perthshire. Origin unclear but probably closely related to 'Slieve Donard' with which there are similarities, but also distinct differences. *IBG, MG9*. ***Notable features:*** *Flowers:* Sky-blue, broadly over-lapping petals. *Emerging leaves:* Possess intense purple-red pigmentation on both dorsal and ventral surfaces. *Mature leaves:* Elliptic, margins distinctly serrate, with shallow teeth. *Fruit capsule:* Slender ellipsoid capsule body bristly, but the sutures between the carpels are bald with no bristles on them, style slender merging gradually with a not very prominent stigma. ***Flowering season:*** Mid-season. ***Compare:*** 'Slieve Donard', 'P.C. Abildgaard', 'Cruickshank', 'Bryan Conway'. ***Availability and cultivation:*** Specialist nurseries; sterile, but propagated readily by division.

25 *Meconopsis* 'Bryan Conway'

Background: A distinct form that came to light in the *Meconopsis* identification and naming trial, named after a donor enthusiast. *IBG, MG1.* ***Notable features:*** *Flowers:* Sky-blue with narrow, ovate, non-overlapping petals, margins wavy. The whole flower has a frilly appearance. *Emerging leaves:* Similar to 'Slieve Donard' being slender, elliptic and densely clothed with long white-tipped hairs and with an absence of any suffusion of red-purple pigment. *Mature leaves:* Long, slender with serrate teeth on the margins, slightly boat-shaped, curved both dorso-ventrally and from end to end. *Fruit capsule:* Long, narrowly ellipsoid and frequently sickle-shaped body, clothed with long bristles. The slender style merges smoothly with the capsule body and tapers smoothly towards the small narrow stigma. ***Flowering season:*** Early mid-season ***Compare:*** 'Slieve Donard' and 'Cruickshank'. ***Availability and cultivation:*** Specialist nurseries; a little difficult to maintain, but well worth the effort.

26 *Meconopsis* 'Blue Butterfly'†

Background: M. 'Blue Butterfly' was selected from plants raised by Liz Young from crossing *M simplicifolia* and *M. baileyi* seed distributed by The Scottish Rock Garden Club. It is basically sterile with much *baileyi* apparent in its parentage. *IBG*ᵠ, *MG54*. **Notable features**: *Posture of plant and flowers: M.* 'Blue Butterfly' has a tall, airy-looking, slender appearance. Strikingly, the flowers, of similar size to those of *M. baileyi*, possess very long pedicels, held high above the false whorls, often "looking down". The petals often become arched upwards. *Emerging leaves:* Elliptic, the base of leaf blade truncate to shortly attenuate, the margins bearing neat dentate teeth. *Mature leaves:* Elliptic, with dentate teeth on the leaf margins. *Fruit capsule:* Ellipsoid body, longer than those of *baileyi* and also the covering bristles are longer and they possess a reddish tinge. **Flowering season:** Mid-season. **Compare:** M. baileyi. **Availability and cultivation:** Rare; readily propagated by division.

27 *Meconopsis* 'Cameron Carmichael'†

Background: A rare cultivar created by Cameron Carmichael, well before 2005, by crossing *M.* 'Bobby Masterton' with *M. baileyi. IBG, MG57*. ***Notable features***: A sterile and handsome cultivar, tall, with large leaves and saucer or shallow bowl-shaped flowers. The latter, around 12 cm in diameter, are substantial, the petals almost circular so therefore broadly over-lapping and mid to sky-blue in colour. The *M. baileyi* in its parentage is clearly indicated by the shape of the leaf-blades which are cordate/truncate at the base, and by the large number of subsidiary flowers borne in axils of leaves below the false whorl. It possesses striking and very large *baileyi*-like fruit capsules. ***Flowering season***: Mid-season. ***Compare***: *M. baileyi*. ***Availability and cultivation***: Very rare, can only be propagated by division. Has proved slow to bulk up.

28 *Meconopsis* 'Clydeside Early Treasure'†

Background: This sterile cultivar was created by Allan Jamieson by crossing *M.* 'Kingsbarns' with *M.* 'Lingholm'. *IBG, MG56.* ***Notable features:*** Consistently the earliest big blue poppy to flower. The flowering stem, relatively short at flower opening, bears just one or two stem leaves and a single flower in the false whorl. *Flowers:* Petals deep blue, narrow and frilly and quite different to those in any other cultivar, opening from long, slender buds. *Leaves:* narrowly elliptical, bearing a few serrate teeth on the margins. *Fruit capsule:* After flowering, the long ellipsoid capsule body, clothed with just a few bristles develops at the apex of the pedicel that increases greatly in length as the flowers mature and fade. ***Flowering season:*** Very early - often the earliest. ***Compare:*** The other very different but early-flowering cultivars, 'Strathspey', 'Great Glen', 'Mildred'. ***Availability and cultivation:*** Specialist nurseries; sterile, readily propagated by division.

29 *Meconopsis* 'Crarae'ᐃ

Background: A highly distinct cultivar that grew in profusion in the garden at Crarae, Argyll and also was found at Kilbryde Castle, near Dunblane, Perthshire. *IBG, MG14*. **Notable features**: *Flowers*: Almost globular in shape, either clear blue or more mauvy-blue. *Emerging leaves*: Paddle-shaped leaf blades, scarcely toothed with only the tiniest of teeth on the margins, suffused with red-purple pigment. Long petioles arch over so that the leaves reach towards the ground. *Mature leaves*: Narrowish, paddle-shaped, set at about 45 degrees to the stem, margins with well-defined shallow serrate teeth. False whorl leaves invariably large. *Fruit capsule*: Ellipsoid body, bristly, including some at the proximal end of the sutures between the carpels, styles long, capped by a well-defined stigma. **Flowering season**: Early-mid season. **Comparison**: None. **Availability and cultivation**: Specialist nurseries; sterile, propagated readily by division.

30 *Meconopsis* 'Crewdson Hybrid' (AM)^Δ

Background: In 1939 Cicely Crewdson found that *M. grandis* had crossed with *M betonicifolia* (now *baileyi*) in her garden to produce a fine plant that became known as "Crewdson hybrid". Originally apparently fertile, it later became sterile. Until relatively recently, seeds wrongly named "Crewdson hybrids" were being distributed by seed companies and seed exchanges. *IBG, MG15.*

Notable features: *Flowers:* Pure deep blue, open frilly cup-shaped. *Emerging leaves:* Suffused with some red-purple pigment, but also possess a brownish tinge, tapering towards the tip. *Mature leaves:* Neat narrow-elliptic leaf blades, margins with shallow, crenate-serrate teeth, taper towards the tip. *Fruit capsule*: Capsule body ellipsoid, densely covered with short bristles, short style, merging with rounded stigma. **Flowering season:** Mid-season. **Compare:** 'Mrs Jebb'. **Availability and cultivation:** Specialist nurseries; sterile, readily increased by division.

31 *Meconopsis* 'Cruickshank'

Background: Discovered amongst several cultivars growing in the Cruickshank Botanic Garden, Aberdeen. *IBG, MG10*. **Notable features**: *Flowers*: Sky-blue, petals broad, rather wavy and overlapping but not as broadly over-lapping as in 'Slieve Donard' or 'Bobby Masterton', whilst broader and less frilly than in 'Bryan Conway'. *Emerging leaves*: Differs from 'Bryan Conway' and 'Slieve Donard, in that the emerging young leaves are intensely suffused with a red-purple pigment, especially on the lower surface. *Mature leaves*: Narrowly elliptical leaf blades with hooked serrate teeth on the margins. Basal leaves become prostrate when mature. *Fruit capsule*: Narrowly ellipsoid body with a long style and slender stigma. Sutures between the carpels completely devoid of bristles. **Flowering season:** Mid-season. **Compare:** 'Bryan Conway' 'Slieve Donard' and 'Bobby Masterton'. **Availability and cultivation:** Specialist nurseries; sterile, propagated by division.

32 *Meconopsis* 'Dagfinn'

Background: Raised by Dagfinn Nilsen in Tromsø from seed (EMAK 473)
collected in the Arun Valley, East Nepal. Introduced to the author by Finn
Haugli of the Tromsø Alpine Botanic Garden. Possibly a natural hybrid
between *M. grandis* and *M. simplicifolia*. IBG^Ψ, MG26. ***Notable features:***
Flowers: Dainty, sky-blue, nodding; scapose, or one to several arising within a
false whorl at the apex of a short flowering stem; pedicels long. *Leaves:* Petioles
long, leaf blades elliptic, with a few dentate marginal teeth on the distal half.
Fruit capsule: Initially strongly deflexed, but becomes strikingly vertical when
mature, knobbly, with stiff bristles; style is long and the stigma large and
rounded. Flowering tends to be in two stages, a lower tier of flowers opening
after the first in which the pedicels lengthen greatly during capsule maturation.
Flowering season: Mid-season. ***Compare:*** 'Houndwood'; they are possibly
conspecific. ***Availability and cultivation:*** Rare; present experience suggests
division can be tricky.

33 *Meconopsis* 'Dippoolbank'†

Background: Alan Brash of Dippoolbank in the Scottish
Borders, grew this distinctive plant over a decade ago
from seed purchased at a garden centre, but he has no
recollection of the name given on the packet. *IBG, MG55*
Notable features: A particularly large, sturdy cultivar up
to 1.5 m in height. Very floriferous, with up to five flowers
arising from the false whorl and more flowers arising in the
axils of a number of the stem leaves below the false whorl.
Flowers: Large, substantial, sky-blue with rounded petals,
wavy around the edges, obtuse at the apex and broadly
overlapping. *Leaves*: Large, bases of the leaf blades of the
basal leaves often truncate or cordate. *Fruit capsule*: Large
capsule body clothed densely with short bristles, style is
broad, the stigma large and prominent. ***Flowering season:***
Mid-late season. ***Compare:*** *M. baileyi.* ***Availability and***
cultivation: Rare, specialist nurseries; not prolific in off-set
production, but easily propagated by division.

34 *Meconopsis* 'Dorothy Renton'

Background: This sterile cultivar from Branklyn Garden, Perth, together with the closely-related 'Stewart Annand' and 'Mervyn Kessell', were probably raised by Dorothy Renton. She created the garden and received wild-collected seed from plant-hunters such as George Sherriff and George Forrest. The parentage of these hybrids is obscure. *IBG, MG20*. **Notable features:** *Flowers:* Blue but often pinkish, shallow bowl-shaped with overlapping petals. *Emerging leaves:* Late, with neatly-toothed margins, slight red-purple pigmentation on the lower surfaces, up-reaching to form a distinctive inverted cone shape. *Mature leaves:* Long, elliptical with distinctive tapering towards the apex. *Fruit capsule:* Capsule body densely covered with short bristles, style broad widening just below the large prominent stigma. **Flowering season:** Mid-season, well ahead of 'Stewart Annand' and 'Mervyn Kessell'. **Compare:** 'Stewart Annand' and 'Mervyn Kessell'. **Availability and cultivation:** Specialist nurseries, but not at present widely grown; sterile, propagated by division.

35 *Meconopsis 'Edrom'*[†]

Background: This cultivar used to be marketed as "Edrom Dark form" from Edrom
Nurseries at Coldingham in eastern Scotland. It is now known simply as 'Edrom'.
IBG$^\Psi$, MG48. Notable features: Flowers: Ranging from deep maroon when tightly
in bud, gradually changing to pale blue, largely forward-facing, four-petalled, petals
ovate, an unusual straight-sided style, tinged with a reddish pigment. The sepals
surrounding the flower before opening are suffused with a near black pigment.
Leaves: Leaf blades wavy with margins indented quite deeply with crenate/serrate
teeth. Both newly emerging and mature

leaves are oblong with a sub-obtuse apex.
The periphery of the young leaves and the
midrib are suffused with a reddish pigment
that is no longer seen as the leaves mature.
Fruit capsule: Carpels with black pigmented
walls are clothed with long bristles.
Flowering season: Mid to late. *Compare:* None. *Availability and cultivation:*
Specialist nurseries; sterile, propagated by division.

36 *Meconopsis* 'Evelyn'△

Background: *M.* 'Evelyn' appeared in Ian Christie's alpine nursery in eastern
Scotland when an unknown visitor left a pot of it at the nursery, but no more is
known of its origin. IBG^Ψ, MG24. *Notable features*: Sturdy, rather stiff, moderately
tall, clump-forming cultivar. *Flowers*: Cup-shaped, forward-facing flower with
thick-textured petals ranging from deep blue to deep purple; petals ovate,
rounded and over-lapping. *Leaves*: Thick-textured both when young and when
mature. Young leaves densely covered with long, dark reddish hairs, and a reddish
pigment suffuses a marginal area around the periphery and along the mid-ribs.
Pigmentation no longer apparent at maturity. *Fruit capsule*: Often bearing one or
more stigma-like projections on some of the sutures joining the carpels, in addition
to the normal apical stigma. Some well-developed seeds are produced, but unlikely
to breed true. Perhaps it should have been placed in the Fertile Blue Group.
Flowering season: Late. *Compare*: None. *Availability and cultivation*: Specialist
nurseries; easily propagated by division.

37 *Meconopsis* 'Houndwood'

Background: It originated as a seedling many years ago in the garden of Houndwood House in Berwickshire and is reported to be a cross between *M. baileyi* and *M. quintuplinervia*, although it more closely resembles *M. simplicifolia* and the much more recent introduction, 'Dagfinn', from Tromsø, Norway. *IBG, MG23.* ***Notable features:*** Many similarities with 'Dagfinn': In both, some flowers are scapose, others arise from within a false whorl. The shape of the petals and nodding posture of flowers is similar, as is the fact that some flowers possess more than four petals. The fruit capsules are similar; the capsule body is knobbly, style long and stigma prominent and rounded. Both 'Dagfinn' and 'Houndwood' are probably crosses of *M. grandis* with *M. simplicifolia*. ***Flowering season:*** Mid-season. ***Compare:*** 'Dagfinn' and 'x hybrida 'Lunanhead' (*M. grandis* x *M. simplicifolia*). ***Availability and cultivation:*** Rare, sterile, propagation by division but this cultivar has been difficult to maintain.

38 *Meconopsis* 'James Aitken'†

Background: James Aitken, the late well-known nurseryman of Perth, was given a plant by Mrs Knox-Finlay of Keillour Castle, Perthshire, that he understood to be the renowned "Betty Sherriff's Dream Poppy". From the appearance and origin of *M.* 'James Aitken' this is very unlikely. Much more probable is that it was a sister seedling of *M.* 'Keillour' which it closely resembles. *IBG, MG52.*
Notable features: Very like 'Keillour' in many respects but rosettes of young leaves of 'James Aitken' emerge later, it blooms later, the flowers are rather more substantial and the plant is taller. *Flowers*: dark blue with pale centres as in 'Keillour', petals rather pleated, small golden anthers that become black soon after flower opening. *Leaves*: oblanceolate as in 'Keillour'. ***Flowering season*:** Mid-late season. ***Compare*:** 'Keillour'. ***Availability and cultivation*:** Not generally available yet; sterile, propagation by division.

39 *Meconopsis* 'John Mitchell'[†]

Background: A plant received as the "original *M. x sheldonii*". It is one of several other long-standing old clones that were received for the identification and naming trial. There are convincing differences from other similar clones and it has now been named *M.* 'John Mitchell', is one of several long-standing old clones that were received for the identification and naming trial. It is clearly closely-related to plants such as 'Slieve Donard', 'Bryan Conway', 'Cruickshank', 'Ormswell' and 'Bobby Masterton'. 'John Mitchell' is a fine, vigorous cultivar very similar to 'Slieve Donard' yet "in the flesh" convincingly distinct. *IBG, MG51.*
Notable features: *Flowers:* Large, sky-blue, broadly ovate petals. *Emerging leaves:* Elliptic, clothed with long, white-tipped hairs. *Mature leaves:* Elliptic, mostly with margins beset with small, crenate teeth (unlike 'Slieve Donard'). *Fruit capsule:* Body elliptic, clothed with long bristles, style long, stigma slender. ***Flowering season:*** Mid-season, differing slightly from 'Slieve Donard'. ***Compare:*** 'Slieve Donard' in particular; also 'Bobby Masterton' and 'P.C. Abildgaard'. ***Availability and cultivation:*** Rare; sterile, readily propagated by division.

40 *Meconopsis* 'Keillour' (AGM)

Background: 'Keillour' originated at Keillour Castle, Perthshire, the home of Major and Mrs Knox-Finlay. Presumed to be have been raised by Mrs. Knox-Finlay. Named in 2002 by The Meconopsis Group. *IBG, MG2*. *Notable features*: *Flowers*: Blue, but a paler shade in the centre, grading to dark blue towards the periphery, not as pleated as in 'James Aitken'; petals ovate, broadly overlapping. Stamens, small, initially golden, soon darkening to near black. *Leaves* Oblanceolate, both when emerging and when mature; stem leaves are not large, and the leaves of the false whorl are particularly small. *Fruit capsule*: Within a group of plants the capsule bodies range in both size and shape from fairly narrow to very broadly ovoid, deeply grooved, with the sutures between the carpels set within these grooves, stigma short and broad, capsule rounded and prominent. *Flowering season*: Mid-season. *Compare*: 'James Aitken'. *Availability and cultivation*: Specialist nurseries; readily propagated by division.

41 *Meconopsis* 'Maggie Sharp' (PC)

Background: A cultivar from Branklyn Gardens, Perth, bought by Maggie Sharp in 1976. Named by The Meconopsis Group in 2002. *IBG, MG13*. ***Notable features:*** *Flowers:* Neat, almost circular, flat-faced, with four overlapping pale blue petals, normally outward facing. *Emerging leaves:* Appear up to a week later than most other cultivars, ascending, narrow, linear/elliptical, intensely suffused with deep purple-red pigment and clothed in abundant long, pale-coloured hairs. *Mature leaves:* Basal leaves narrower and more parallel-sided than in most other cultivars; the leaf blades possess a prominent white mid-rib at all stages of development and the margins are neatly and evenly toothed. *Fruit capsule:* Capsule body narrow, oblong-elliptic, densely clothed with long bristles, noticeably parallel-sided, grading smoothly into the slender style and thence to a narrow stigma; sutures partially bristly. ***Flowering season:*** Early mid-season; ***Compare:*** 'Louise', 'Harry Bush' and 'Mildred' (all FBG). ***Availability and cultivation:*** Specialist nurseries; by division, but not been found to be the easiest.

42 *Meconopsis* 'Mervyn Kessell'

Background: One of three cultivars (the others are 'Dorothy Renton' and 'Stewart Annand') with obscure parentage from Branklyn Gardens, Perth, that were undoubtedly raised by Dorothy Renton, who, with her husband created that garden. She had access to wild-collected seed from plant-hunters such as George Forrest and George Sherriff. *M.* 'Mervyn Kessell' was named by The Meconopsis Group, in honour of our co-founder who sadly died prematurely in 2001. *IBG, MG19*. *Notable features*: One of the very latest to bloom. *Flowers*: Purple on opening, later becoming blue. Petals ovate, overlapping, largely smooth–edged; pedicels shortish. *Emerging leaves*: Very late (the latest), thick-textured, clothed densely with dark hairs appearing almost black. *Mature leaves*: Lengthen to become broadly oblong-elliptic, with an ascending, slightly outward-reaching posture and neatly distributed marginal teeth. *Fruit capsule*: Body small, clothed densely with short bristles, style short and broad, stigma dark and large. *Flowering season:* Late. *Compare*: 'Dorothy Renton' and 'Stewart Annand'. *Availability and cultivation:* Specialist nurseries; sterile, readily propagated by division.

43 *Meconopsis* 'Mrs Jebb' (AGM)

Background: 'Mrs Jebb', probably arose in a batch of 'Crewdson Hybrid' seedlings when the latter was still fertile at Jack Drake's nursery. It was given to Mrs. Jebb of Brooklands in Dumfriesshire, passed to Ireland and then back to Scotland where it was more widely distributed as 'Mrs Jebb' via Margaret and Henry Taylor. *IBG, MG16.* *Notable features:* Like 'Crewdson Hybrid', 'Mrs. Jebb' is a little shorter than most other cultivars. *Flowers:* Shallow saucer-shaped, borne on short pedicels, petals deep blue, crisp, pleated, orbicular and broadly overlapping. *Emerging leaves:* Suffused with red-purple pigment, but also have a brownish tinge. *Mature leaves:* Narrow-elliptic with neat crenate teeth on the leaf margin and with a sub-obtuse tip. *Fruit capsule:* Short ellipsoid body covered densely with short bristles, merging with a very short, broad style connecting to an almost globular stigma. *Flowering season:* Mid-season. *Compare:* 'Crewdson Hybrid'. *Availability and cultivation:* Specialist nurseries; readily propagated by division.

44 *Meconopsis* 'Ormswell'†

Background: 'Ormswell' was most probably a sister seedling of the cross made by Dr Curle in about 1935 between *M. baileyi* and *M. grandis* ssp. *grandis* which also produced 'Slieve Donard'. It was associated with Edrom Nursery, but is now rare. *IBG, MG60*. *Notable features:* Unlike 'Slieve Donard' that grows readily, 'Ormswell' appears to be lacking in vigour and difficult to grow. *Flowers:* Blue, with ovate, broadly overlapping petals. *Leaves:* Emerging leaves are erect, narrowly elliptic, suffused with red-purple pigment, clothed densely with short hairs and with small serrate teeth on the leaf blade margins. The red-purple pigment is no longer seen in the mature leaves. *Fruit capsule*: Sutures between the carpels are devoid of bristles, unlike those of 'Slieve Donard'. *Flowering season:* Mid-season. *Compare:* 'Slieve Donard'. *Availability and cultivation:* Rare; sterile, tricky to bulk up.

45 *Meconopsis 'P.C. Abildgaard'* (AGM)

Background: 'P.C. Abildgaard' was received in 1999, subsequently recognised
as distinct, and this name ratified in 2007. Professor P.C. Abildgard was founder
of the university in Copenhagen in the garden of which Troels Juhl had noticed
it. *IBG, MG12*. *Notable features:* Very robust, floriferous and with handsome
foliage. *Flowers:* Similar to 'Slieve Donard' and 'Bobby Masterton', but the petals
of the sky-blue flowers are not quite so broad and overlapping. Four to 7 flowers
arise within the false whorl, often with further single flowers in the axils of the
upper stem leaves. *Emerging leaves*: Densely clothed with long white-tipped hairs.
Mature leaves: Conspicuously oblong-elliptic, the leaf blade margins indented
with evenly distributed serrate-dentate teeth. *Fruit capsule:* Capsule body
ellipsoid, clothed with long bristles, merging smoothly with the slender style and
similarly, the latter with the stigma. *Flowering season:* Mid. *Compare:* 'Slieve
Donard' and 'Bobby Masterton'. *Availability and cultivation:* Specialist nurseries;
sterile, a vigorous clone, readily propagated by division.

46 *Meconopsis* 'Peter Cox'†

Background: A cultivar seen growing in Peter Cox's garden at Glendoick, Perth; prior to that it was grown at Kilbryde Castle, near Dunblane, but its earlier origins are not known. *IBG, MG58*. *Notable features:* A tall, elegant cultivar with a number of unusual features. *Flowers:* Deep blue, initially the flowers are rounded, but the petals lengthen a little to form more open, deeper cup-shaped flowers, the petals with a wavy edge and the flowers tend to be nodding. *Emerging and mature leaves:* Rather broadly elliptic with several neat distally facing dentate teeth occurring along the edge of the margins of the distal two-thirds of the leaf blades. *Fruit capsule:* Body ellipsoid, clothed densely with prominent ginger bristles; abrupt demarcation occurs between it and the broad style, and between the latter and the rounded, prominent stigma. *Flowering season:* Mid to late. *Compare:* None. *Availability and cultivation:* Rare; sterile, readily increased by division.

47 *Meconopsis* 'Slieve Donard' (AGM)

Background: In about 1935, Dr Curle of Edinburgh crossed *M. baileyi.* (then known as *M. betonicifolia*) with *M. grandis* ssp. *grandis* and succeeded in raising several seedlings, one of which was subsequently introduced to Slieve Donard nursery in Northern Ireland, whence it acquired its name. The name was later changed to *M* x *sheldonii* 'Slieve Donard', the epithet x *sheldonii* reflecting its hybridity and parentage. *IBG, MG8.* ***Notable features:*** *Flowers:* Sky-blue, with broadly overlapping petals and with a prominent long and slender style, merging gradually into a rather slender stigma. *Emerging leaves:* Rosettes, noticeably upright and slender, covered with long, white-tipped hairs. Suffusion with red-purple pigmentation is usually absent. *Mature leaves:* Elliptical with marginal teeth absent or minute. *Fruit capsule:* Slender and ellipsoid, with long, slightly white-tipped, spreading bristles. ***Flowering season:*** Mid-season. ***Compare:*** *M.* 'Bobby Masterton', 'P.C. Abildgaard', 'John Mitchell' and 'Ormswell'. ***Availability and cultivation:*** Specialist nurseries, quite widely available; outstanding sterile cultivar, easily propagated by division.

48 *Meconopsis* 'Stewart Annand'

Background: Named after Stewart Annand, the first National Trust head
gardener at Branklyn Garden, Perth. One of three closely related cultivars (the
others are 'Dorothy Renton' and 'Mervyn Kessell') almost certainly raised by
Dorothy Renton, who, with her husband created the garden, and who had
access to wild-collected seed sent by plant-hunters such as George Forrest and
George Sherriff. However, the parentage of these hybrids is obscure. *IBG, MG21*.
Notable features: A late-flowering, tall, slender plant. *Flowers:* Blue, petals
ovate, somewhat overlapping. *Emerging leaves*: Notably late to emerge, elliptic,
ascending, thick-textured, some suffusion of red-purple pigment. *Mature leaves*: Elliptic, markedly in both basal and stem
leaves, elongated and tapering towards the tips. *Fruit capsule*: Ellipsoid body clothed densely with short, ginger bristles,
the style short and broad, and the stigma rounded. *Flowering season:* Late, but not as late as 'Mervyn Kessell'. *Compare:*
'Dorothy Renton' and 'Mervyn Kessell'. *Availability and cultivation:* Specialist societies; readily propagated by division.

49 *Meconopsis* 'Willie Duncan' (PC)^Δ

Background: 'Willie Duncan' was raised in 1972 by Willie Duncan, Gardens Superintendent at Silverburn Park, Fife from purported *M. grandis* seed from the Scottish Rock Garden Club Seed Exchange. The Meconopsis Group ratified the name in 2001. *IBG^Ψ, MG17*. *Notable features:* Certain features suggest *baileyi* in the parentage. *Flowers*: Deep blue or mauvy-blue. Clusters nestle on short pedicels within the false whorl. Deeply cup-shaped with broadly over-lapping petals which appear humped due to arching towards the proximal end. Subsidiary flowers often occur in the axils of the upper stem leaves. *Emerging leaves*: Flat, firm-textured, distinctive light green colour, clothed with short ginger hairs, margins of leaf blades indented with neat crenate-dentate teeth. *Mature leaves*: large, oblong-elliptic, margins of leaf blades indented with neat crenate-dentate teeth, retaining a lightish green colour. *Fruit capsule*: Ovoid body, clothed with short bristles, the styles long, stout and twisted, the stigmas prominent. *Flowering season:* Mid to late. *Compare:* None. *Availability and cultivation:* Specialist nurseries; propagated by division. Seedlings not true to type.

50 *Meconopsis* x *finlayorum*[†]

Background: A plant seen in 2001 growing in a bed by the front door of Keillour Castle in Perthshire, is probably the hybrid *M.* x *finlayorum* that was reported to have been raised by Mary Knox-Finlay at Keillour Castle. *M.* x *finlayorum* is the hybrid created by crossing *M. quintuplinervia* with *M. integrifolia*. Alan Innes, the gardener, donated it for the identification and naming study. *IBG, MG100.* **Notable features:** A neat, short plant about 40–50 cm tall. *Flowers*: Pale mauvy blue (in my experience), wavy, ovate petals, deeply cup-shaped and mainly nodding. *Leaves*: Flowering stem arises from within the rosette of elliptic basal leaves, terminating with a false whorl from which one to several flowers arise. *Flowering season:* Early to mid-season. **Compare:** None. **Availability and cultivation:** Rare; sterile. Without care and attention it dwindles, but should thrive with care.

51 *Meconopsis* x *hybrida* 'Lunanhead'†

Background: *M* x *hybrida* 'Lunanhead' is a hybrid re-made most recently by Leslie Drummond by crossing *M. grandis* with *M. simplicifolia*. *M* x *hybrida* was first made by F.C. Puddle at Bodnant Garden in north Wales. *MG59, IBG*Ψ.
Notable features: Tall, slender rather elegant cultivar. *Flowers:* Shallow cup-shaped with ovate, smooth-edged, non-overlapping mid blue petals. Two to four flowers, borne on long pedicels, arise from the false whorls. *Leaves:* Elliptical, with neat, serrate teeth indenting the margins. Stem leaves narrowly elliptical and well-spaced, with the false whorl leaves relatively large. *Fruit capsule*: Long and narrowly ellipsoid body, clothed fairly densely with bristles, merging smoothly with the long style, in turn, merging with a long, narrow, yet prominent stigma. ***Flowering season:*** Mid-season. ***Compare:*** 'Dagfinn' and 'Houndwood'.
Availability and cultivation: Specialist nurseries; readily increased by division. Any seed-raised plants should not be labelled 'Lunanhead'.

Section D: Fertile Blue Group

Section D: Fertile Blue Group

This Group comprises plants believed to be hybrids (not species) but which are fertile producing viable seeds. The most significant one is the now well-known *M.* 'Lingholm', together with a number of cultivars that have been selected from it. *M.* 'Lingholm' originated, by chance, in the garden of Drs Digby and Roger Nelson in Cumbria, in north-west England in the 1960s. Apart from these there are several others placed in this group, e.g. 'Kingsbarns'.

When two different species are cross-pollinated the hybrid formed is in most cases sterile. This is because the chromosomes in two different species are not identical and this will prevent the pairing process that occurs during normal cell division to form the gametes; this results in a sterile plant. Occasionally, however, during cell division of a sterile hybrid there may be in addition a doubling of the chromosomes that results in a fertile hybrid being produced.

If *M. grandis* is successfully crossed with *M. baileyi,* the resulting hybrid is called *M.* x *sheldonii.* One fertile hybrid believed to have arisen from this cross is *M.* 'Lingholm' which produces capsules full of viable seeds. There is evidence to suggest that *M.* 'Lingholm' arose as a result of chance doubling of its chromosomes during seed development, resulting in it producing seeds that are fertile. The chromosome number found in 'Lingholm' supports this view (unpublished findings). It is likely that the x *sheldonii* cultivar in which this doubling occurred might well have been *M.* x *sheldonii* 'Slieve Donard' as this was growing in the Nelson's garden in the early 1960s when M. 'Lingholm' first appeared.

Top: A single flower from the original clone of *M.* 'Lingholm'.

Above: Taken many years later in a nursery bed in south-west Scotland where *M.* 'Lingholm' was growing for seed production.

Left: The garden in Cumbria where *M.* 'Lingholm' first occurred.

Plants resulting from such seeds are variable in their genetic make-up and this results in variation in morphological features. Some of these plants have been selected by gardeners for particularly desirable features, propagated vegetatively by division and given cultivar names of their own. Examples are shown below.

Photographs: 1) *M.* 'Louise' 2) *M.* 'Mop-head' 3) *M.* 'Lingholm' 4) *M.* 'Harry Bush'

52 *Meconopsis* 'Lingholm'

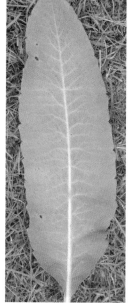

Background: 'Lingholm' originated from a plant in the garden of Digby and Roger Nelson in Cumbria in the early 1960s. They had purchased the plant from Jack Drake's Inshriach nursery. It is quite a variable cultivar that has yielded a number of distinct plants with desirable features, many of which have been given their own name. *FBG, MG33*. **Notable features:** *Flowers:* Sky-blue, shallowly bowl-shaped nodding or forward-facing flowers with four broadly overlapping petals. *Emerging leaves:* Elliptic, ascending, densely covered with long white-tipped hairs. *Mature leaves:* Fairly broad, elliptic, usually with shallow, rather irregularly distributed teeth on the margins. *Fruit-capsules:* Fertile, reliably producing capsules filled with viable seed. Plump, ellipsoid body, with long bristles, usually conspicuously white-tipped, style long and slender, stigma also slender. **Flowering season:** Mid-season. **Compare:** 'Slieve Donard', 'Bobby Masterton' and 'P.C. Abildgaard', all of which are sterile. **Availability and cultivation:** Garden centres, nurseries, seed exchanges; can be raised from seed or by division.

53 *Meconopsis* 'Harry Bush'

Background: Purchased by nurseryman, Harry Bush, at a garden opening of the Sherriff's garden at Asceavie in Angus in the early 1970s and passed on to nurseryman, Graeme Butler and thence to the identification trial. *FBG MG36*. **Notable features:** *Flowers:* Sky blue, shallowly bowl-shaped with 4 overlapping, ovate petals. Usefully, it consistently flowers a few days later than other Fertile Blue Group cultivars. *Emerging leaves:* densely clothed with striking white-tipped hairs. *Mature leaves:* leaf blades elliptic, neat with evenly serrate-dentate teeth on the margins. *Fruit capsule*: Most striking are the capsules clothed densely with long, ginger bristles having prominent white tips. **Flowering season:** Mid to late. **Compare:** Other examples of FBG clones attributed to the rather variable cultivar 'Lingholm'; 'Louise', 'Mildred'. Its later flowering readily distinguishes it from "other Lingholms". **Availability and cultivation:** Specialist nurseries; although fertile, it must be propagated vegetatively in order to be labelled 'Harry Bush'.

54 *Meconopsis* 'Mop-head' (AGM)

Background: Selected by Liz Young from seedlings of purported *M. grandis* seed from The Scottish Rock Garden Club seed exchange in the 1980s. Liz nick-named it 'Mop-head'. Its name was ratified by The Meconopsis Group in 2007. Probably or possibly not a selection from 'Lingholm'. *MG37, FBG,* but only occasional seeds are formed. *Notable features: Flowers:* Deep blue, exceptionally large (up to 23 cm across), a few with 5 petals, petals broadly ovate and over-lapping. Flowers open just above the mature leaves. Then the pedicels lengthen greatly during fruit-capsule maturation. *Emerging leaves:* Amongst the earliest to emerge. Leaves elliptic, markedly erect, densely clothed with long hairs, darkish green in colour. *Mature leaves:* Broadly elliptic with repand margins. Prominent flower buds emerge just above the leaves on short flowering stems. *Fruit capsule:* Large body, clothed with stout bristles, large twisted style and large stigma. *Flowering season:* One of the very earliest. *Compare:* 'Lingholm' and other Fertile Blue Group cultivars. *Availability and cultivation:* Specialist nurseries; readily propagated by division.

55 *Meconopsis* 'Ballyrogan'[†]

Background: *Meconopsis* 'Ballyrogan' was bought, with this name, from Gary Dunlop in Ireland in 1997. It is clearly a fine, long-lived selection from *M.* 'Lingholm'. Although fertile, as with other named Fertile Blue Group cultivars. it is to be treated as a clonal cultivar as it cannot be assumed that seedlings will come exactly true to type. *FBG, MG92.* **Notable features:** Well-formed flowers of a lovely shade of blue, a robust plant, with neatly toothed leaves, and distinctive fruit capsules with long ginger bristles with white tips. *Flowering season:* mid-season, although usefully a little later than some forms of *M.* 'Lingholm'. **Compare:** Other selections from *M.*' Lingholm'. **Availability and cultivation:** Specialist nurseries; readily propagated by division.

56 *Meconopsis* 'Louise'△

Background: A cultivar of *M*. 'Lingholm' that was selected as distinctive by The Meconopsis Group member, Les Newby, and named after his grand-daughter. The Meconopsis Group confirmed the name in 2007. *FBG*ᵛ, *MG35*. ***Notable features:*** *Flowers:* Flat-faced and of a paler shade of sky-blue than almost all other cultivars. Petals are very broad so that the overlapping of the petals may give an almost square appearance. *Emerging leaves:* Slightly suffused with red-purple pigment. *Mature leaves:* Elliptic-oblong leaf blades edged with neatly indented serrate teeth. *Fruit capsule:* Densely clothed with long, white-tipped bristles, prominent rounded stigma. Very little, if any viable, seed produced. ***Flowering season:*** Early mid-season, ahead of other "Lingholms". ***Compare:*** 'Harry Bush', 'Mildred', 'Maggie Sharp' (all paler-coloured forms) and other "Lingholms". ***Availability and cultivation:*** Specialist nurseries; although fertile, producing some seeds, it must be propagated vegetatively to retain this cultivar name.

57 *Meconopsis* 'Mildred' (PC)^Δ

Background: Mildred Thompson (centre in photograph) noted this distinctive cultivar in a batch of seedlings she raised from seed given to her after an open day garden visit in Auchtermuchty, Fife, a number of years ago. It appeared that it was a 'Lingholm' seedling. The Thompsons maintained the original plant by division and The Meconopsis Group named it 'Mildred' in 2011. *FBG, MG 34*. *Notable features*: *Flowers*: An arresting turquoise-blue with four broadly overlapping petals. Amongst the earliest to flower. *Emerging leaves*: Amongst the earliest to emerge. Young leaves clothed densely with conspicuous white-tipped hairs. *Mature leaves*: Oblong-elliptic with neatly serrate teeth on the margins, a conspicuous whitish mid-rib and slightly more silvery green than most cultivars. *Fruit capsule*: Capsule body clothed densely with long, ginger white-tipped bristles. *Flowering season*: One of the earliest. *Compare*: 'Lingholm', 'Louise', 'P.C. Abildgaard', 'Slieve Donard', and 'Bobby Masterton'. *Availability and cultivation*: Specialist nurseries; readily propagated by division. Fertile, but variable such that seedlings are not to be labelled 'Mildred'.

58 *Meconopsis* 'Kingsbarns'

Background: 'Kingsbarns' is clearly quite distinct within the Fertile Blue Group. James Cobb explains in his book "Meconopsis" (1989) that "a single plant of *M. x sheldonii* produced viable seed in quantity. The resulting progeny, which is also highly fertile, very variable in form and colour is clearly the result of a back cross which could have been either *M. betonicifolia* (now *baileyi*) or *M. grandis* since both were nearby". *FBG, MG38*. *Notable features: Flowers:* A single flower (four, 5 or 6-petalled) arises from the false whorl at about 30cm. Flowers, blue or blue-mauve, lateral-facing. Petals ovate, wavy, giving an open "wind-mill" effect. *Leaves, emerging and mature:* Narrowly elliptical, clothed densely with short hairs, virtually devoid of marginal teeth. *Fruit capsule*: Large, ellipsoidal or globular, glabrous filled with large, viable seeds. Pedicels lengthen greatly during capsule maturation. *Flowering season:* Early to mid-season. *Compare:* Contrast with 'Lingholm' and compare with *grandis ssp grandis* 'Himal Sky'. *Availability and cultivation:* Specialist nurseries and society seed exchanges; by division (very long-lived) or from seed.

Section E: White forms

Section E: White forms

Most of the plants dealt with in this book are the blue-flowered big perennial blue poppies. In addition to the white form of *M. baileyi*, that is, *baileyi* 'Alba', there exist a few white-flowered or very pale cream-coloured cultivars that are described here.

59 *Meconopsis* 'Kilbryde Castle White'† (shown opposite) and 'Ascreavie White'† (above)

Background: 'Kilbryde Castle White' was a white flowered form from Kilbryde Castle, Dunblane, but its earlier origin is unknown. Very similar 'Ascreavie White' was growing in the Sherriff's garden at Ascreavie, Angus, for more than 45 years (a photograph shows it there in 1969). *WF, MG61* and *MG62*. **Notable features**: Both are tall, with white flowers, borne on pedicels that soon after opening become unusually elongated. *Flowers*: Almost identical, but in newly opened 'Kilbryde Castle White' the petals are frequently streaked with a few blue lines that subsequently fade. In 'Ascreavie White' this only occurs rarely. *Emerging leaves*: Young foliage emergence is early. Leaves elliptical and upreaching, clothed with long, whitetipped hairs. *Mature leaves*: Elliptic, the distal two-thirds of the margins, coarsely, and rather unevenly, indented with serrate-dentate teeth. Fruit capsule: Long ellipsoid body, clothed densely with deflexed bristles. *Flowering season*: Mid. *Compare*: 'Marit'. **Availability and cultivation**: Specialist nurseries; sterile, readily propagated by division.

60 *Meconopsis* x *beamishii* (shown opposite) and *Meconopsis* x *sarsonsii* (above)

Background: Both *M* x *sarsonsii* and *M*. x *beamishii* are well-documented hybrids that have been in cultivation for many decades resulting from crossing *M. integrifolia* with *M. baileyi* and with *M. grandis*, respectively, and featuring characteristics of *baileyi* and *grandis*, respectively. But there is some confusion at present over their correct identities. From investigations over several years, it appears that x *sarsonsii* is rare, but is growing well at Branklyn Garden, Perth. *M*. x *beamishii* appears to be less rare and plants from three different sources are growing in the author's garden. In both cultivars the petals are a very pale cream, but it has proved difficult to show this shade accurately in photographs which usually indicate that they are white. As a result, in the pictures here, there is one accurate-colour photo of x *sarsonsii* (taken by Steve McNamara) and none of x *beamishii*. The other photos, in which the flowers appear white, are included to show other features of these cultivars. ***Notable features: M*. x *beamishii:*** The broadly overlapping ovate petals are much longer than in x *sarsonsii*, the fruit capsule body is also much longer and the bristles on the capsules are deflexed. The margins of the leaves are coarsely dentate. ***Notable features: M*. x *sarsonsii:*** Overall the flower looks very like *M. baileyi*. This includes the rounded ovate petals resulting in a saucer-shaped flower, the short, ovoid fruit capsule body densely clothed with short, spreading bristles, short style and rounded stigma. The shape of the base of the basal leaves is reputed to be cordate, but it is observed that there is a range from cordate to attenuate.

It has proved very difficult to obtain a satisfactory set pictures for these two cultivars. They must therefore be regarded as part of "work in progress" and are limited to:

1) *M. x sarsonsii* with reasonably good colour reproduction.
2) *M. x sarsonsii* showing the *M. baileyi*-like form of the flower.
3) *M. x sarsonsii* showing the *M. baileyi*-like flowers and fruit capsules.
4) *M. x sarsonsii* showing the *M.baileyi*-like shape of the young leaves.
5) Thought to be *M. x beamishii* showing the *M. grandis*-shaped flowers.
6) Thought to be *M. x beamishii* showing the *M. grandis*-shaped flowers.
7) Thought to be *M. x beamishii* showing the leaves of a different shape to those of *M. x sarsonsii*.
8) Thought to be *M.* x *beamishii* showing the leaves of a different shape to those of *M. x. sarsonsii*.
9) Fruit capsule thought to be *M. x beamishii*.

All the flowers, except in photo 1 appear white, but in reality are a very pale cream – a colour which has proved very difficult to achieve in photographs, even by several experts.

61 *Meconopsis* 'Marit' (AGM)

Background: Marit Espejord of Tromsø, north Norway, crossed *M.* 'Lingholm', and *M.* x *sarsonsii*, using seed from Thompson and Morgan and a Swedish seed exchange, respectively; this resulted in three sterile plants with one selected as *M.* 'Marit'. The name was ratified by The Meconopsis Group in 2008. It received an AGM in 2013. *WF, MG25*. *Notable features:* An attractive plant with broadly elliptic leaves possessing neat serrate-dentate teeth on both the basal leaves and handsome stem leaves. *Flowers*: Early-flowering, white, with four broadly over-lapping, ovate, wavy-edged petals, nestling in a cluster at the apex of the false whorl. *Emerging leaves*: Early to emerge. Densely clothed with long ginger hairs, the ginger appearance gradually fading. *Fruit capsule*: Short ellipsoid body, densely covered with long, ginger, white-tipped bristles. *Flowering season:* Early to mid-season. *Compare:* 'Kilbryde Castle White' and 'Ascreavie White'. *Availability and cultivation:* Specialist nurseries; sterile, propagated readily by division.

62 *Meconopsis* 'Edrom White'†

Background: A white cultivar from Edrom Nursery. It is currently (2015) listed as *Meconopsis* 'Edrom White' in the Edrom Nursery catalogue, previously it was listed as *M. grandis* 'Alba'. *WF,MG88*. *Notable features*: "*M. grandis* ssp. *grandis*-like" features are evident when observing the basal, stem and false whorl leaf characteristics, and the flower. The fruit capsule is clothed with long spreading bristles. It is uncertain whether it sets seed. *Flowering season:* Mid-season. *Compare:* Other white cultivars. *Availability and cultivation:* Specialist nurseries, but rare; propagated by division. Having dwindled considerably, it is currently building up nicely again in the author's collection.

63 Three recently acquired cultivars: *Meconopsis* 'Steve McNamara'†, 'Cally Purple'† and 'Keillour Violet'†

These three lovely purple cultivars have only recently been selected as being distinct and have yet to be ratified by The Meconopsis Group, so at this stage only their background is given. However, the photographs below suggest they are worthy of naming.

M. 'Steve McNamara' has been selected from a batch of 'Lingholm' seedlings purchased a number of years ago for Branklyn Garden. This one proved to be a robust plant, the flowers a strong purple rather than blue. It has been named for Steve McNamara, the retiring Garden Manager and Head Gardener at Branklyn, as a tribute for all he has done during his time at the garden since 1997, including his enthusiasm for the big perennial blue poppies. The collection of big blue poppies at Branklyn was granted Plant Heritage National Collection status in 2006. This cultivar will, of course, only be propagated by division to validly carry this name.

M. 'Cally Purple' was selected some years ago by Michael Wickenden from within a large planting of normal blue-flowered 'Lingholm' being grown for seed production. It is clearly distinct from 'Steve McNamara' and is a clonal cultivar that has been carefully increased vegetatively for distribution to *Meconopsis* enthusiasts.

M. 'Keillour Violet' arose in the garden of Stuart Pawley. Its origin is rather uncertain. Although there is some doubt about it, it probably arose from a viable seed from within a fruit capsule of *M*. 'Keillour'. But 'Keillour Violet is very different in appearance from its near name-sake and it produces fruit capsules packed with viable seed. So this plant seems to present a mystery!

Photographs: 1) *M*. 'Steve McNamara' 2) *M*. 'Steve McNamara' 3) *M*. 'Cally Purple',
4) *M*.'Keillour Violet', 5) *M*.'Cally Purple', 6) *M*.'Keillour Violet'

64 *Meconopsis* 'James Cobb'†

Background: James Cobb crossed *M. napaulensis* (of hort*) or *M regia* hybrid with *M. grandis* in 1984 resulting in this cultivar. *WF, MG110*. ***Notable features:*** This cultivar has proved perennial and long-lived, but is not widely grown at present. It is evergreen with attractive pale green densely hairy leaves. The flowers are pale yellow, but it has proved to be not very floriferous, not flowering at all in many years. ***Flowering season:*** Mid-season. ***Compare:*** None. ***Availability and cultivation:*** Very rare, sterile, but readily propagated by division.

* 'of hort' indicates that the plant is a horticultural form of *M. napaulensis* that may not be identical with the species growing in the wild.

Cultivation and Propagation

This section is written in the light of over 35 years of experience of growing the big perennial blue poppies in central Scotland. Most of my experience has been in growing the sterile hybrids rather than growing plants from seed.

Cultivation

Undoubtedly success with *Meconopsis* has a lot to do with climate. *Meconopsis* come from the mountainous regions of the Himalayas, western China and Tibet. These areas are cold, with snow cover in winter, and experience monsoon conditions with high rainfall during the summer growing and flowering season. They clearly thrive in gardens where the climates more nearly approximate those of their native habitats. Thus they flourish better in the cooler and wetter parts of northern Britain than in the warmer and drier south. Other areas which suit *Meconopsis* well include coastal British Columbia, Alaska, Iceland, and northern Europe such as Tromsø in the north of Norway. However, with knowledge of their needs and an undertaking to manipulate to some degree the micro-climate of the beds where they are to be grown, success with *Meconopsis* is achievable in less favourable areas. One instance can be seen at Wakehurst Place, Sussex, in the bog-garden area, where *M. baileyi* appears to flourish. I hope that with the information given here more gardeners will be encouraged to gain satisfaction from growing these lovely plants.

This account of cultivation will start with a plant ready to plant out into the garden, either a pot-grown specimen or one lifted from the open-ground. Early spring or late summer is a suitable time to do this when there is a good chance that it will become well-established before the onset of the more stressing weather conditions of summer and winter, respectively. For potted plants, it is preferable to plant out into the garden before plants become root-bound, but even if they are, they respond well once transplanted into the open ground. *Meconopsis* are not particularly deep-rooted and therefore do not reach down to great depths in the soil and my experience is that they can be moved around the garden quite readily, if this is done with care, ensuring minimum root-disturbance and watering well until re-established.

Even though not being very deep-rooted, it is important to prepare the soil well. The aim should be to produce a nutrient-rich soil, at least the depth of the tines on your garden fork, with a friable, crumbly texture and with reasonable drainage. This is achieved by digging the soil thoroughly and by adding liberal amounts of organic matter e.g. garden compost, leaf-mould and well-rotted manure. Producing a good soil is clearly more arduous for gardeners with a heavy, clay-based soil, but it can be done. Some growers maintain that *Meconopsis* are very greedy feeders and need as much manure as can be supplied. I have not felt the need to add large amounts of manure to our soil. This may be due to its inherent high nutrient level – it was a farmed field 30 years ago. Occasionally I have applied some inorganic fertiliser granules and on one occasion, slow release fertiliser granules, but have not been convinced that they were of benefit. However, whenever I do any replanting, I make sure to enrich the soil, again digging well and adding more garden compost and some manure if available. It is striking to observe the beneficial effect of such measures.

After planting, and at other times as convenient, a mulch of garden compost, well-rotted manure or bark chippings is placed around the plants, taking care to avoid covering the central crowns. However, recently an experienced grower informed me that she had discovered that it is not necessary to avoid covering the crowns when she mulched her beds in autumn with well-rotted leaf-mould; there were no deleterious effects and it saved her a lot of time! The purpose of mulching is to help retain high moisture levels in the soil and high air humidity in spells of hot weather, as well as improving nutrient levels and soil texture. In the occasional heat-waves we experience, it is also important to irrigate the beds which I do by overhead irrigation. A seep-pipe (a hose-pipe with small perforations to yield a slow and constant release of water on the surface of the soil) is another good method to retain adequate moisture levels. Probably the worst 'enemy' of *Meconopsis* is excessive heat and a dry atmosphere during summer droughts, so different from their homeland monsoon. Losses in the south of England appear to be associated with long, hot summers, e.g. the infamous summer of 1976, and even here in Scotland one feels the need for irrigation if a hot, dry spell sets in.

Meconopsis thrive best in dappled shade in an open site, the aim being to give them enough sun-light, but to avoid them being scorched during hot, sunny spells, These conditions can be provided by growing in the vicinity of deciduous trees and shrubs which will also give shelter from summer gales. Strong winds can damage the leaves and may bend the flowering stems. *Meconopsis* thrive less well very close to the base of trees, despite the fact that this may give them the dappled shade they relish. This is presumably due to competition with tree roots for water during dry spells. As the big blue poppies are deciduous, with the leaves dying down in winter, they need no overhead protection.

It is often maintained that *Meconopsis* require an acid soil. There is evidence that this in not so. They can grow well in both acid and alkaline soils, although it is probably necessary to avoid extremes of both conditions. Further, despite many statements to the contrary, I have shown that the colour of the flowers is not affected by the pH (acidity or alkalinity) of the soil.

Probably important if the soil is on the heavy side and liable to water-logging is the addition and digging in of coarse grit. If water-logging threatens to be a problem raising the soil level of the bed slightly by the addition of more soil components can be a satisfactory solution. I have taken these precautions and by and large the plants thrive in our cool, not particularly sunny, summers. Although not grown in truly boggy soil, surprisingly, even in wetter parts of the garden, the *Meconopsis* flourish, so I think they are possibly not as averse to winter wetness as is sometimes reported - but this tolerance of winter wet may be related to the overall amount of winter rainfall: in areas of higher rainfall, succumbing to water-logged conditions may be more of a problem.

When growing well, plants can become congested with multiple shoots growing very close together within a clump. It is then desirable, even important, to split clumps every two or three years. It is then desirable to replant the "splits", into soil that has been rejuvenated with fresh garden compost and other organic material, preferably into a new area of the garden, and then watered well until re-established.

On the topic of planting, an interesting observation, seen several times by myself and by at least one other enthusiast, is that sometimes a clump, having grown and flowered very well in a given year will have "overdone it" and be much reduced in the next. However, if cared for by enriching the soil around it with compost, the following year it is restored to full vigour and flowering.

If, however, a plant seems truly to be ailing, it is invariably possible to rescue it by lifting it, separating out healthy off-sets, potting them up individually in good compost and then tending them carefully in a frame or greenhouse until re-established. So the message is, do not despair if you think a plant is going to die – invariably it can be rescued!

A further interesting observation is that occasionally, at the end of the season, an apparently truly dead flowering stem will bear a cluster of healthy new leaves, well above its base. This can be detached and potted up when it will develop into a new plant.

I have not myself grown the big blue poppies in pots, but know that this can be done with great success as seen in plants grown by Sharon Bradley for the award-winning stands of The Meconopsis Group at Gardening Scotland (*www.gardeningscotland.com*). Sharon uses large 15–25 litre pots, splits the plants every year or so before they become root-bound, and re-pots using a friable compost with added slow-release fertiliser. This method has the advantage that, as the plants are in moveable pots, she can be flexible about where she places them.

Propagation

Most of the plants described in this book are sterile hybrids and therefore the only means for increasing numbers is by vegetative propagation. At present, this means establishing new individuals from existing plants by division, although in future, other means may be possible. Of course, for the fertile taxa that produce viable seed, raising from seed is an option.

Vegetative propagation

Vegetative propagation may be achieved by carefully lifting a mature plant and splitting it into two or more pieces and replanting. If a number of new plants is required, the lifted plant may be carefully teased or split apart by hand and separated into pieces (off-sets) each comprising a newly formed bud preferably with some associated roots. Even offsets with no roots, but with the base-plate at the bottom end of the bud intact, or partially intact, should be successful. The off-sets are then potted into good compost, watered and kept in sheltered conditions, e.g. a glass-house, polytunnel or cold-frame, and not allowed to dry out until fresh roots and shoots have developed when the new plants can be planted out or otherwise distributed. One mature clump can yield a variable, but sizeable number, of off-sets (10, even 20 or 30). The compost should be a friable one. Now that using peat may be a problem, I use a commercially available multipurpose compost and add horticultural grit or perlite for added friability for the young roots to grow into, and a slow-release fertiliser is also added.

The root-systems of the big perennial blue poppies are of two main types, the clump-formers and the rhizomatous forms. (See illustrations on page 86.) In the clump-formers the new buds are concentrated around the base of the current year's dying-down flowering stems. In the rhizomatous forms, underground stems grow out from the base of the flowering stems with buds developing at intervals along the length of the rhizomes and at their apices. Each of these buds is a potential new plant. Buds have even been seen to develop occasionally on a dead flowering stalk.

Young shoot

Base of current year's flower stem

Young shoot

Young shoot

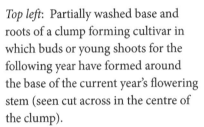

Top left: Partially washed base and roots of a clump forming cultivar in which buds or young shoots for the following year have formed around the base of the current year's flowering stem (seen cut across in the centre of the clump).

Top right: Another clump-forming cultivar showing the base of the dying or dead current year's flowering stem, together with developing young buds (shoots) around and just below it.

Centre: The washed base of a rhizomatous cultivar, showing the roots and several short rhizomes growing out from the base of a current year's flowering stem with buds developing at the apices of the rhizomes. New buds also arise at intervals along the length of the rhizomes, but this is not shown clearly here.

Bottom: Separated and washed divisions of a clump-forming cultivar. Further buds are developing at the base of each division that will develop into rosettes of basal leaves and flowering shoots the following year.

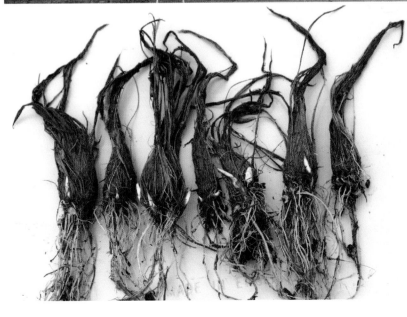

There are various times of the year that growers recommend vegetative propagation should be performed. One is early spring about the time of leaf emergence when the new buds are about to put on active growth. These plants will yield the maximum number of developed off-sets and be ready for the new season's growth. After flowering, further development takes place with the growth of new shoots above ground, and dormant buds just below ground level, for the following year's growth and flowering. Therefore late summer or early autumn is also a good time to undertake division when the current year's new growth has been maximised, and there is still sufficient warmth for new growth to occur before the onset of winter. The big perennial blue poppies are very hardy and do not appear to be adversely affected by winter frosts. Some people advise splitting them after flowering. To obtain the greatest number of new plants, this has the disadvantage of not having allowed time for the development of the maximum number of removable new shoots at the base of the flowering stem. Also it is more difficult to avoid the ill-effects of water loss while the new roots are developing at this warmest time of the year.

Raising from seed

As abundantly recorded in this book, most of the big perennial blue poppies are sterile hybrids that for the most part do not set viable seed. However, the species *grandis*, *baileyi* and the hybrid *M.* 'Lingholm' do produce capsules full of viable seeds. *Meconopsis* have the reputation, regarded by some as justifiable and not by others, of being difficult to propagate from seed. Different growers have a range of views on how to achieve success. On the website of The Meconopsis Group, *www.meconopsis.org.* (follow the link to Cultivation, Propagation and Raising from seed) there are the views of a number of experts on how they grow big perennial blue poppies from seed. The following is a summary of these recommendations.

1. After harvesting, store seed, cleaned and dry in a sealed container in a domestic fridge. Storage in a cool room is also satisfactory. By and large seeds from commercial sources can usually be expected to be less viable than home-collected seeds, and those from the specialist society seed exchanges, but even so often prove very satisfactory.

2. The type of compost used for seed germination is not too critical. A peat-based one is most usually used. An important feature is for it to have high air porosity. The incorporation of a lot of grit or perlite to ensure minimum root damage when pricking out is particularly important.

3. Sowing freshly harvested seed will give a high germination rate, but has the disadvantage of the need to over-winter plants when still small. Therefore sowing seeds from December to February is usually recommended. Seeds should be placed thinly onto the surface of moist compost in trays or plastic pots. Water the pots from below (avoids seed disturbance), or from above with a fine spray. Leave uncovered, or cover the seed with several millimetre of fine grit or a little sieved compost.

4. There are various recommendations for the next step. Leaving pots in freezing conditions for a week or two appears to be desirable. Then the pots are brought into warmer conditions such as leaving out-of-doors, on a window-sill, in a greenhouse (around 15^{0}C) with or without a heated bench or in a cold-frame. At Holehird Gardens (*http:// holehirdgardens.org.uk*), a dew-point cabinet is used (*http://www.twowests.co.uk*) with great success. Never allow the surface to dry out, especially after germination has taken place. Germination takes two weeks to several months, sometimes occurring in the second year.

5. Damping-off can be a problem. The probability of this occurring can be minimised by sowing thinly and keeping the pots in a well-ventilated situation. Very dilute fungicide applied on first observing the problem can help.

6. Prick out seedlings at the two- or three-leaf stage. Avoid damaging the stem by handling the leaves only. Transfer gently to the same light compost, avoiding compaction. Keep in a shady place until growth has resumed. Keep the plants growing actively, and re-pot before the pots become root-bound. It is important not to let the plants suffer a check in growth.

7. Transfer to larger pots or into the garden when large enough. Depending on the climate, this is done in summer, late summer-autumn or the following spring.

Harvesting and cleaning seeds

Seeds are best collected from the fruit capsules as soon as the latter are ripe. The capsules become brown in colour and the valves at the apex of the capsule split open so that ripe seed is readily shaken out. Good seed must be separated from aborted seeds, any bristles etc. (See illustrations below.) Some people do this by placing the seed on a sheet of paper and winnowing off the dross. I find an excellent method is to use a large enamel plate for this process. By tipping the plate, and by tapping it, the good seed drops to the depression in the plate near the bottom edge, from where it can readily be collected, leaving behind the dross. The seeds should then be packeted, labelled and stored in a lidded plastic box in a fridge. However, I find that storage of seed for a few months in a cool room (in central Scotland!) is not detrimental to seed viability.

Meconopsis 'Lingholm' fruit capsules
filled with plump viable seed.

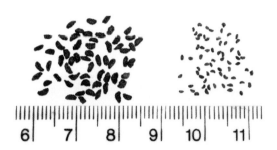

M. 'Lingholm' and *M. baileyi* showing the
unmistakably different sizes of seeds.

Valid naming

Meconopsis are notorious for hybridising in gardens, this, after all, being the source of our many cultivars of the big perennial blue poppies. In my own experience, however, I have not found hybridisation amongst my collection to be a problem, especially as most of the plants are sterile. But there are some cultivars that frequently, or occasionally, produce some capsules with some viable seed. In order to avoid the possibility of producing plants of a given named cultivar which do not meet the description of that cultivar, it is important not to distribute seed labelled with the name of the purported cultivar. For example, *M.* 'Willie Duncan' consistently produces a few viable seeds, but we have found these not true to type. Therefore collections from this cultivar must be labelled "*M.* ex 'Willie Duncan' and <u>not</u> distributed to seed exchanges etc. as *M.* 'Willie Duncan'.

Future work

As the result of the work carried out by The Meconopsis Group over the last fifteen years, a large number of cultivars have been named and their morphology, development and vigour described in detail, but many aspects need further research – a few areas are outlined below. Perhaps one of the most important is to clarify the phylogenetic relationships within the species, subspecies and cultivars. Such work requires cytological and molecular techniques. Some work has been carried out using Rapid Amplified Polymorphic DNA markers to study species of *Meconopsis* in the wild e.g. *M. quintuplinervia, paniculata and simplicifolia*. It is possible from this work to construct dendrograms, i.e. phylogenetic trees that indicate the relationship between the taxa examined. It would be very helpful to have comparable data for the cultivars described here.

While many of the cultivars described are sterile, others are fertile but to varying degrees. The latter may depend to a greater or lesser extent on environmental conditions, but also on genetic factors. Therefore a detailed cytological examination of the chromosomes including their number might help to understand the varying fertility observed. Because *Meconopsis* has a large chromosome number it is not easy to obtain exact counts, and also to pick out individual chromosomes based on their overall shape.

Petal colour in the big perennial blue poppies is a very important, both aesthetically and as a factor in identification. It varies during the development of the flower and may be influenced by environmental conditions e.g. nutrients, pH, temperature. A few studies have been made of the pigments that contribute to the colours observed, but no comprehensive studies have yet been made.

It has often been stated or assumed that *Meconopsis* need to be grown in an acid soil (i.e. with a low pH), although there is some evidence that this is not so. However, it would be desirable if this could be rigorously investigated.

Further species and fine cultivars may come to light. One species that is currently being investigated is the possible recent introduction of *M. betonicifolia* from Yunnan. This may prove to be a hybrid. At present it is being circulated with the nickname "*M.* 'Alaska*" and "*M.* MGS#3" and has not been covered in this book. It would also be desirable if *M. simplicifolia*, at one time quite widely grown became once more readily available in cultivation.

Some work has already been done, notably by Leslie Drummond, on re-creating the man-made hybrids reported in the past (see Cobb, 1989, pp. 105-111). It would be desirable if this work were to be further extended.

Further reading

Taylor, George (1934) *An account of the genus Meconopsis,* New Flora and Silva Ltd. For decades the "bible" on the genus. Out of print.

Taylor, George, *Meconopsis*, Waterstone,1985 – a reprinted edition of the above, out of print, but still available.

Cobb, James, L.S. (1989) *Meconopsis,* Christopher Helm and Timber Press. Out of print, but still available. An account of the genus that has greatly helped to popularise these plants, including guidance on growing them.

Grey-Wilson, Christopher (2014) *The Genus Meconopsis, Blue poppies and their relatives,* Kew Publishing, Royal Botanic Gardens, Kew. An extensive and authorative revision of the genus *Meconopsis*. Extensively illustrated with fine photographs from many sources.

Terry, Bill (2009) *Blue Heaven: Encounters with the blue poppy,* Touchwood Editions (2009)

Terry, Bill (2012) *Beyond Beauty: Hunting the wild blue poppy ,* Touchwood Editions (2012)

These two beautifully written books tell of Bill Terry's passionate love of *Meconopsis*, both growing them in his garden and an account of an adventurous trip with a party to Tibet to see them in the wild.

A number of articles on *Meconopsis* may be found in various gardening journals, including relatively recent issues of The Royal Horticultural Society's journal, *The Plantsman* (and *New Plantsman*), The Scottish Rock Garden Club's journal, *The Rock Garden*, the Alpine Garden Society's journal, *The Alpine Gardener* and *Sibbaldia*, a journal from The Royal Botanic Garden Edinburgh.

There is also much information on the web-site of The Meconopsis Group: *www.meconopsis.org* and also on: *www.meconopsisworld.com*

Glossary

acute: sharp, sharply pointed - opposite of obtuse

anther: part of the stamen containing the pollen

apex: tip of an organ

attenuate: gradually narrowing over a distance

axil: the angle between the stem and leaf

bristle: a stiff pointed hair

bud: immature shoot

capsule: a dry, dehiscent fruit composed of two or more united carpels, opening when ripe in these plants, by slits at the apex

carpel: a unit consisting of the ovary, style and stigma

cauline: arising from the stem, e.g. from the flowering stem

clone: a group of plants resulting from vegetative propagation from a single parent and therefore genetically identical to the parent

conspecific: same taxon, species, cultivar

cordate: having a deep notch at the base of a leaf-blade (lamina) giving the leaf a heart-shape

cultivar: a cultivated variety of a species or hybrid

deflexed: bent abruptly downwards

dentate: prominently toothed with acute projections pointing outwards

distal: furthest from place of attachment – opposite of proximal

ellipsoid: elliptic in outline in a 3-dimensional body

elliptic: broadest at the middle with two rounded ends

entire: smooth, unbroken by teeth

false whorl: in these plants the circle of several stemless leaves encircling the apex of the flowering stem (peduncle) from within which a cluster of flowers typically arise

fertile: able to reproduce sexually

fruit capsule: develops from the ovary, comprising three parts: the larger capsule body, the style and the stigma.

glabrous: free of hairs

herbaceous: composed of soft, non-woody tissue

hybrid: a cross between two species

inflorescence: part of the plant which bears the flowers, but excluding unmodified leaves (= flowering stem).

lamina: leaf blade = expanded part of a leaf which attaches to the petiole

monocarpic, flowering once only, then dying

oblanceolate: narrowly obovate and tapering to a point at the apex

oblong: (of a plane shape) longer than broad, with the margins parallel for most of their length

obovate: egg-shaped 2-dimensionally with the broadest part near the apex

obtuse: not pointed, blunt – opposite of acute

off-set: a lateral shoot used in propagation

ovary: the lower part of a carpel (or carpels) which contains the ovules

ovate: egg-shaped, 2-dimensionally, with the wider part below the middle

ovoid: egg-shaped, 3-dimensionally, with the broader part below the middle, or nearest the base

ovule: a structure which after fertilisation, develops into a seed.

pedicel: stalk of an individual flower

peduncle: in this context, the flower stem from the ground up to the false whorl

perennial: living for many years. We have used this term instead of the more accurate term "polycarpic"

petiole: the leaf stalk, the narrow part of a leaf between its base and the leaf blade (lamina)

phenotype: the physical characteristics of an organism, influenced by both genetic and environmental factors

pollen: the small grains that contain the male reproductive cells of the flower

polycarpic: fruiting many times, not dying after first fruiting – opposite is monocarpic. The big perennial blue poppies are, more accurately, termed "polycarpic"

proximal: nearest to place of attachment – opposite distal

repand: with a slightly sinuate margin

rhizome: a root-like stem lying horizontally underground bearing buds or shoots and adventitious roots

scapose: having a scape, that is a leafless stalk arising from the ground which bears one or more single flowers

serrate, toothed like a saw, with acute and angled teeth pointing towards the apex

sessile: without a stalk

shoot: an elongating stem

spreading bristles: extending horizontally

stamen: the male organ of the flower consisting of a stalk (filament) and anthers (pollen sacs) that bear the pollen

sterile: unable to reproduce sexually

stigma: the apex of the style on which pollen grains alight and germinate

style: the often elongated part of the carpel that bears the stigma at its tip

suture: a seam or line of joining

synonym: another name for the same taxon that is now invalid according to the ICBN that has been superseded by a later name.

taxon: a general term denoting a named group, e.g. variety, species, genus

truncate: ending abruptly, appearing cut off

whorl: a set of similar organs arranged in a circle around a central axis

Meconopsis-rich Gardens
and Sources of Plants

It is expected that readers will wish to see a range of the plants pictured in this book "in the flesh" and to obtain some to grow in their own gardens. In this section is listed a number of "Meconopsis-rich gardens" and information on sources of plants.

Meconopsis-rich gardens:

Most of the "Meconopsis-rich" gardens featuring both the big perennial blue poppies (and other members of the genus), are located within Britain, notably in the north of England, Scotland and Northern Ireland. Many of the gardens are listed below. Most of them usually have big blue poppies for sale, although sometimes this is restricted to the flowering season. See the appropriate web-sites for further details. Other gardens featuring these plants may be found by further searching the internet. Private gardens may also be found by searching through "Scotland for Gardeners" by Kenneth Cox, published by Birlinn (2014), (*www.birlinn.co.uk*) and "Scotland's Gardens", published annually: *www.scotlandsgardens.org*.

1. Branklyn Garden, Dundee Road, Perth, Perthshire: An exceptional garden caring for a Plant Heritage collection of the big perennial blue poppies and other members of the genus, sited attractively around the garden. *www.nts.org.uk/ BranklynGarden.*

2. Holehird Gardens, Windermere, in The Lake District: Another exceptional garden with a well-maintained Plant Heritage collection of the big perennial blue poppies, sited both in an area dedicated to them and in other beds around the garden. *www.holehirdgardens.org.uk.*

3. RHS Garden, Harlow Carr, Harrowgate, North Yorkshire: An extensive number of the cultivars of big perennial blue poppies, enchantingly replanted following the RHS trial of these plants in this garden for the Award of Garden Merit, 2010-2013. *www.rhs.org.uk/gardens/harlow-carr.*

4. Explorers: The Scottish Plant Hunters Garden, Pitlochry, Perthshire: Quite a wide range of cultivars in the Himalayan section of the garden. The plan is to extend this to a National Collection. *www.explorersgarden.com.*

5. Attadale Gardens, Wester Ross in the Scottish Highlands: A large selection of the cultivars attractively sited in different areas around this extensive and beautiful garden in an equally beautiful landscape. *www.attadalegardens.com.*

6. Edrom Nurseries, Coldingham, Eyemouth, Berwickshire: A wide range of big perennial blue poppies planted in a woodland setting. *www.edrom-nurseries.co.uk.*

7. Royal Botanic Garden Edinburgh, together with their regional gardens, especially Dawyck and Logan. Noted for strikingly extensive beds of big perennial blue poppies. *www.rbge.org.uk* and follow the link: "The Gardens".

8. Glendoick Gardens, Glendoick, Glencarse, Perthshire: Big perennial blue poppies enticingly planted in beds within this world-famous rhododendron/woodland garden. *www.glendoick.com/Visit-Glendoick-Gardens.*

9. Cluny House Gardens, Aberfeldy, Perthshire: A famous woodland garden, created and developed over more than 65 years and noted for its collections of Himalayan plants including *Meconopsis. www.clunyhousegardens.com.*

10. *Inshriach, Aviemore, Inverness-shire:* The famous alpine nursery, located in an attractive woodland setting and founded by Jack Drake in the late 1930s. Jack Drake was largely responsible for the propagation and early commercial distribution of the big perennial blue poppies, and the nursery is still going strong. *www.inshriachnursery.co.uk*

11. Crarae Garden, Minard, Inverary, Argyll: A lovely National Trust for Scotland woodland garden, noted, amongst many other plants, for its "river of blue poppies" *www.nts.org.uk/Property/Crarae-Garden*

12. Cally Gardens, Gatehouse of Fleet, Castle Douglas, Kirkudbrightshire: A nursery with a very large stock, noted for the planting in its complementary garden for the plants that it sells, amongst them big perennial blue poppies. *www.callygardens.co.uk*

13. *Dalemain Gardens, Penrith, Cumbria:* A fine 5-acre garden, particularly noteworthy in the present context for the wild garden with its spectacular and memorable large beds of *Meconopsis* 'Dalemain' a member of George Sherriff Group. I do not know of another garden planted so extensively with a cultivar of this Group. *www.dalemain.com*

14. *Rowallane Gardens, Saintield, Co. Down, Northern Ireland:* A large garden including fine displays of big perennial blue poppies in the rock garden wood. *www.nationaltrust.org.uk/rowallane-garden*

15. *Mount Stewart, Newtonards, Co. Down, Northern Ireland:* Another large garden with fine displays of big pernnial blue poppies. *www.nationaltrust.org.uk/mount-stewart.*

16. *Timpany Nurseries, 77. Magheratimpany Road, Ballynahinch, Co. Down, Northern Ireland: Meconopsis* both in the garden and for sale in the nursery. Tues-Sat 10.00 till 7.30. *www.timpanynurseries.com*

17. *Beryl McNaughton, "Tynebank", east of Edinburgh, by appointment only:* A lovely garden with a wide range of big perennial blue poppies. *beryl@macplants.co.uk*

18. *Alpine Garden Schachen, Munich Botanic Garden:* The first three weeks of July are the best time to visit. It is a 3-hour walk up to the Alpine Garden from the Wanderparkplatz (hiking parking area) near Schloss Elmau via the Wetterstein Alm along the forestry road called the Koenigsweg. More information can be found at *www.botmuc.de/en/info* - and follow the link: Garden

19. *Jardins de Metis/Reford Gardens, Quebec,Canada:* Elsie Reford started to create this outstanding garden in 1926. She successfully introduced *M. baileyi* as seeds and it still thrives there in spectacular fashion, said to be the largest planting of *M. baileyi* in the world. *www.jardinsdemetis.com.*

Sources of plants:

Reliable nurseries with a special interest in *Meconopsis* are the following:
1. MacPlants: *www.macplants.co.uk*

2. Edrom: *www.edrom-nurseries.co.uk*

3. Kevock: *www.kevockgarden.co.uk*

4. Glendoick: *www.glendoick.com/Visit-Glendoick-Gardens*

5. Christies Alpine Nursery: *www.ianchristiealpines.com*

6. Cally Gardens: *www.callygardens.co.uk*

7. Timpany Nurseries: *www.timpanynurseries.com*

See also the Meconopsis-rich gardens above, many of which have plants on sale. Also see The RHS' 'Plant Finder'.

There are many other nurseries and garden centres selling big perennial blue poppies, especially the commoner ones, that is *M. baileyi* (until a few years ago known as *M.betonicifolia*) and the now frequently available *M.* 'Lingholm', but it is worth pointing out that one should be wary, lest as sometimes happens, they are incorrectly labelled.

These lists are relevant to the present time (2015), but, of course, over time, will become outdated.

Index